The Complete Spindle Turner

Spindle Turning for Furniture and Decoration

The Complete Spindle Turner

Spindle Turning for Furniture and Decoration

Hugh O'Neill

The Crowood Press

First published in 1998 by
The Crowood Press Ltd
Ramsbury, Marlborough
Wiltshire SN8 2HR

British Library Cataloguing-in-Publication Data
A catalogue reference for this book is available from the British Library

ISBN 1 86126 059 8

Line illustrations by Andrew Green.

Photographic Acknowledgements
All photographs by the author except those on pages 9, 99 (top) and 118
which were supplied by Hapfo Pollards Ltd.

Typefaces used: text, New Baskerville and Garamond; headings, Optima Bold.

Typeset and designed by
D & N Publishing
Membury Business Park, Lambourn Woodlands
Hungerford, Berkshire.

Printed and bound by Paramount Printing Ltd, Hong Kong.

Contents

PREFACE

It was only half in jest that the club member said: 'Good Heavens, I thought you could only make bowls on woodturning lathes!' The event was a spindle-turning demonstration that I was giving to a woodturning club.

You can understand the reaction, in that the explosion of interest in turning in recent years has manifested itself in a vast outpouring of bowls, of every size, shape and description; in fact bowl turning has even been elevated to the status of being a creative art form in its own right. At craft fairs more and more turners have had stands, and many seem to offer only bowls – and it is not difficult to see why, since the bowl provides a platform for the display of the many wonderful colours and dramatic figuring to be found in the timbers now available. But therein also lies a problem, because often the wood is so spectacular that the piece sells despite the fact that the design is awful, and that the workmanship and finish is often appalling.

The trouble is, that making a bowl on a lathe is just too easy: with a few minutes' instruction, anyone can do it, and if you make a mistake, you just carry on, modify the shape a little, and rub away the errors with abrasives. This is not really skilful. But who cares? Indeed, many admiring relatives will be very pleased with their little gifts of 'Uncle Jack's work'!

Most of the vast army of woodturners are hobbyists, and only a small handful of practitioners make a full-time living from it. The rest get immense pleasure from the few hours a week they spend beavering away in their garden workshop or garage corner and to them the ease of bowl turning is part of its attraction; therefore many remain at this level of involvement. Others however, although lifelong amateurs, become extremely talented and produce work of the highest order and of both innovative and classical design; freed from commercial pressures, they have the time to 'push the boundaries' in more experimental endeavour.

Unfortunately, the interest demonstrated by the general public in buying woodwork is very small, and the average craft-fair punter's concept of what turned wood is worth is distressing. Certainly turning at its present level of appreciation in the marketplace will support only the existing few full-time craftsmen and therefore many of those who dream about a new, creative career soon abandon this ambition. Also, most of the turners you meet are on the mature side. Some started at school, but others only began to develop an interest as retirement loomed. Unfortunately, woodwork has disappeared from the timetable of many schools today, and almost all have sold off their lathes; in fact there cannot be more than half-a-dozen people in the country who are actually qualified to teach turning, with the result that aspiring turners, both amateur and embryo professionals, now have to seek tuition elsewhere. Sometimes they are lucky and find an evening class run by a local professional, but most have to rely on guidance from a friend who is already an enthusiast. There are many established practitioners who offer two-day introductory courses, and some, even though they

Fig. 1 Spindles come in all sizes. There is no such thing as waste wood to the spindle turner. These bowl offcuts will make light pulls and lace bobbins.

may hold no qualification, are good. Here you may get a taster of various aspects of turning and learn the basics of tool handling. There is also now an increasing number of instructional videos, and of course there are books.

One very interesting fact emerges when you look at the programme for many of the two-day courses; and it is certainly reinforced by most of the books on basic techniques: they all start with spindle, or 'between-centres' turning. Probably the first thing that most students make is a simple turning tool handle. They probably then go on to practise various shaping cuts on a spindle – but often the work piece is purely an exercise with no other function. Only then does the student move on to 'better things': they start to make bowls! It may be this way of progression that has, at least partially, stimulated the idea that bowl turning is the higher end of the turner's art; it is certainly the ease with which it can be done that has made it such a favourite. But how about challenging this concept?

Yes, I say! Between-centres turning is the best thing to start with – but this is *not* because it is the easiest. It is because it requires better tool control and requires more precise skills. It also clearly exposes, and therefore teaches, what wood grain and figure and tool presentation are all about; and it also employs more, and more different tools and different cuts than does face-plate or bowl turning.

And it goes on from there. Later on, as you get further into turning, it is only occasionally that you turn a single spindle; usually you are making multiples, or at least pairs: pairs of candlesticks, pairs of cruets, fours of legs, scores of stair banisters – and now you really are into a different league, because once you have made the pattern piece, all the others have to be exact copies. You have to work to precise dimensions, and to copy those dimensions from one to the rest; a single error on any one of the copies and it has to be scrapped, or used on another job. You cannot hide your error or moment of inattentiveness by cutting it away and modifying the design as you do on bowls.

Many bowl turners use abrasives extensively to obtain a good finish – indeed there are some timbers such as the Australian Burrs, with which there is no reasonable alternative. But generally in spindle turning, abrasives are not a good idea, primarily because the moment you try to clean up a little untidy tooling, the crisp detail which is so much an essential of a good spindle, becomes softened and blurred.

And let's go a little further, we have to consider applied decoration such as carving, because as well as now appearing more frequently on bowls than it did in the past, we also find much more of it in spindlework: thus the ability to produce fluting and twists is an essential element in the spindle-turner's armoury.

So my contention is, that much greater skill is required in spindle turning than ever there is in making bowls – and this becomes doubly true if we include boxes and goblets, for both include substantial elements of spindle or between-centres turning, and the components have to be made to very accurate sizes and fits. Certainly if you want to see the ultimate demonstrations of the turner's art, look not to bowls, but to those pieces that involve many different spindle-turned elements: spinning wheels, towel rails, button-turned chairs, platform rocking chairs, and many, many more.

This book is dedicated to all spindle turners. I hope it will attract more to the ranks, and will convince the many 'bowlies' who are now bored with the limited prospects of that particular field, that there is indeed a life after bowls! – and that spindles, not bowls, should be considered as the pinnacle of the turner's art.

There are a number of people whom I would like to thank for their help in producing this book: Jamie Wallwin and Allan Batty who first taught me to turn a spindle; and Ian Durrant whose innovative off-centre work, referred to later, opened new avenues of adventure. Also Ray Key and the Association of Woodturners of Great Britain who provided many years of inspirational contact with the world's best; and the several editors of *Woodworker*, *Good Woodworking* and *Woodturning* who encouraged me to write about the subject. Lastly thanks to my own students whose work provided some of the illustrations in this book; and to my wife, Eve, who has always been encouraging and only occasionally complained about the trail of shavings through the house!

WHY TURN SPINDLES?

This book is not full of projects: it is concerned with skills, and it is aimed at three target groups. Thus the first part is intended for the beginner who is about to start turning, and is a tutorial guide to basic spindle turning; hopefully it will provide a supporting text to those following a training course in basic turning skills. The second target is the furniture maker who wishes to produce their own decorated spindle elements for furniture, be it fine chair legs or elegant lamp columns. The third group comprises the dedicated bowl turners (as indicated in the Preface), and here the aim is to try to convince them that there are more demanding skills that they can develop when they become bored with bowls.

To take an overview of the processes of turning and carving decorated spindles, there are three broad avenues which can be addressed. First we must defend our case for being interested in the skills of spindle turning; we must then consider the nature of the field, and clarify a few definitions; and thirdly we need to reflect upon some of the major implications.

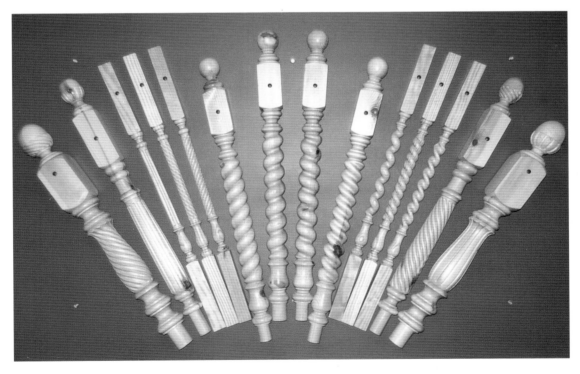

Fig. 2 A group of spindles turned on a Hapfo lathe.

I believe that we can defend a commitment to spindle turning as follows: first and foremost concerns the skills which are involved – namely, you have to be accurate. On a spindle you cannot make a mistake, particularly if it is the second of a pair! Whereas if you make a mistake in turning a bowl you can simply modify your design and proceed as though nothing had happened. The second point is related, in that most spindles have a purpose, unlike bowls, the majority of which are made just to produce something pretty in wood. The purpose will dictate some design constraints and, much more important, will probably predicate certain specific measurements, thus once you have designed the piece, you will then have to make it to the designed measurements. It is in this requirement, above anything else that true turning skills are required.

Spindle turning has always been recognized to be the best form of turning on which to learn basic skills and tool control. You use almost all the standard tools that any turner ever uses, and you have to use them properly, as mistakes are easy to make and become immediately apparent – and as we have already stated, they cannot then be rectified.

BASIC TOOLS

The basic tool of all turning is a chisel, a tool with a handle at one end and a sharp cutting edge on the end of a long blade. Chisels come in many guises: some we call gouges, because they make scooping cuts and therefore have a rounded sectional blade; otherwise the kernel of the turner's tools can be considered to be the flat chisel we know as a skew chisel. This chisel and its use presents us with all the fundamental elements and concepts of shaping wood on a lathe. Essentially it is the tool from which all other turning tools have developed. In its simple form it is used extensively upon spindles, but it

has had to be modified into other shapes in order to work in tight corners and on curved surfaces such as bowls. Understanding the skew chisel and how to use it optimally is the real key to all good turning; indeed, skill with the skew is fundamental to spindle turning, and the best of the experienced bowl turners all acknowledge that they, too, cut their teeth on it.

With a skew you can learn all there is to know about cutting wood – in fact with a skew you *have* to learn it, because it demands accuracy, a thorough understanding of slicing and peeling, delicacy of touch, and a keen feeling for grain orientation. It is very sensitive to defects in the wood, and while 'figure' may be vital to the visual effect it bestows to the wall of a bowl, its true meaning and implication as a (usually wild) variation in the grain and the lie of the timber fibres hits you with full force if you try to turn it as a spindle.

DEFINING SPINDLE TURNING

We do have a problem here, and some readers will already be getting irritated. In fact it is a semantics issue. So far I have used the phrases 'spindle turning' and 'bowl turning' and there is a school of thought that differentiates between the two forms by calling them 'between-centres' and 'faceplate' turning. However, does it really matter? Although I mix them in this text; my justification for tending more to the former is this: basically, many spindles are turned between centres – although we will later touch upon methods of mounting spindles that are not strictly 'between centres' for example the making of goblets and boxes.

Then again, is a cup chuck – often used by spindle turners – really a 'centre'? And what of the end grain hollowing out of a box? What complicates the case even further is

Fig. 3 Turning between centres: spindle turning!

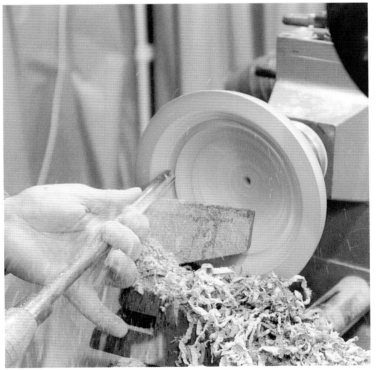

Fig. 4 Face-plate turning: a bowl in pear wood.

that there are stages in the process of turning big vases and large bowls from unruly, out-of-balance burrs, when we use between-centres turning as the safest method for some of the more tricky operations. To cap it all, all bowls produced in medieval times were made on pole lathes and were always turned 'between centres'.

For this text then, 'spindles' are those elements or items that are longer than they are broad; they are fundamentally but not exclusively turned between centres (of whatever form); and they have grain running along the length of the lathe's axis. Of course boxes and goblets also meet most of these criteria, but they do involve other elements such as working into end grain. 'Boxes' are only briefly dealt with here as they should be considered as a very specialist area of turning in their own right.

'Decorated' is used to signify that the profile and/or the surface has been modified to give eye appeal.

SO WHAT DOES THE SPINDLE TURNER MAKE?

Spindles always have a purpose, and we can identify four categories; and we will be exploring these in greater depth when we consider design aspects. For the time being, let us say first that spindles can be pure decoration, a prime example of these being the split turnings used to edge or decorate pieces of classic furniture. They feature on many long-case clock carcasses, and appear as beadings on table edges and similar.

Secondly, spindles can support, and it is here that we see the widest application: this category includes the legs of stools, chairs and tables; the longer legs of standard lamps, also pole screens, four-poster beds and lecterns; and the feet of chests and wardrobes.

Their third function is to keep a framework in its required shape without using solid board, such as the frame of a cot, the rim of a galleried bowl, tapestry frames, hour-glasses, embroidery lamps, the stretchers under chairs, banister spindles, and a host more although today, architectural columns and banister spindles are probably more decorative spacers than functional supports.

The fourth purpose is functional in its intrinsic nature, and the range is legion, including rolling pins, handles, fishing priests and otters, pens, lace bobbins, garden dibbers, honey 'spoons', salad servers, spindles and shafts, and a vast range of other treen items.

There are also compound spindle-turned articles where more than one function is covered, such as the spinning wheel; this constitutes one of the ultimate tests of the spindle-turner's art, since the elements all make structural, spacing and functional contributions.

Such a list only scratches the surface and is given just to indicate the breadth of the subject we loosely call spindle turning. Many of the items listed, and those of a similar nature, are relatively simple and in fact require only minimal turning skills. Some, however, require high levels of turning and then complex furniture-making skills; there are many early chairs and some period beds that were constructed entirely of turned elements and were made by a craftsman who was as much a turner as he was a cabinet maker. Indeed, today there is a move to institute training in turning as just one part of a wider training in cabinet work.

THE WIDER IMPLICATIONS OF SPINDLE TURNING

This now raises a number of fundamental issues that may be significant to many readers, and which have profound implications in a wider context. It may be that here we can account for the 'bowl fixation' of so many turners: perhaps theirs really is the 'easy option'. Let us explore this skill/difficulty question a little further. In the list of the potential outputs from the spindle turner's workshop we can see that only a few spindles exist in isolation; thus although some are simply decorative ornamentation, more frequently they have a definite practical function, meaning that they are often going to be a part of something else. You can fashion a bowl and make it look beautiful by working to a good design and by using strikingly figured wood, and you do so purely because you think of it as a one-off, decorative piece (a view not always shared by potential buyers, who often have a more utilitarian outlook).

On many of the occasions that we are producing a decorated spindle, however, what we are doing is only a part of a larger process. Thus, even if the spindle is merely a candlestick or a standard lamp column, it will not exist totally and singly in its own right, because it will certainly have a base, and maybe even a top disc, and although these elements may be turned between centres, they are much more likely to be turned

off a face plate, a screw chuck or a pin chuck. So, do we then make just the spindle part and leave the rest to someone else?

The spindle turner has two options: to some people it is enough to remain simply a turner. There are those who make a reasonable living as jobbing turners, and much of their output is spindles and columns for local builders; in fact there is a better living to be made from 'between-centres' turning as a sub-contractor than there is from face-plate work.

Alternatively, the turner may make the whole piece themselves, and this means

Fig. 5 An early English, spindle-turned chair.

that they also have to have furniture-making or cabinet-making skills. In fact the turner with a strong spindle bias – unless he is operating as a jobbing sub-contractor – is much more likely to be a furniture maker, as were the bodgers and turners of old. So one of the implications of developing an interest in spindles is that you may have to extend your skills to anything from bodger to full-blown cabinet maker.

So when we consider turning spindles 'in the round', so to speak, we cannot set up a totally arbitrary boundary around the definitions of spindles or 'between-centres' turning; neither should we confine ourselves to traditional lathes and conventional turning tools.

MORE RECENT DEVELOPMENTS

Spindle turning has been around a lot longer than has face-plate turning, even the early bowls, platters and drinking vessels were produced 'between-centres', the implication being that tooling and methods were therefore well established centuries ago. For this reason we have not seen the same proliferation of tools that has flooded into the much younger art of bowl turning, where we see two or three new tools appear each year. Many have been gimmicks to con a burgeoning market; although it has to be admitted that a number have broken important new ground.

The between-centres world has not, however, stood still and there have been useful developments; for example some of the newer chucking methods, and some sizing and copying aids do have a lot to offer. In times past, and still to some extent today, decoration on legs and table edges was applied with carving tools and a scratch stock – a profile ground, flat, steel scraper blade mounted in a wooden handle. Today

the router has taken over from moulding planes and scratch stocks, and we must therefore consider what place it has or could have in the turner's total armoury – I consider its role to be significant. We will be examining some of these important developments later in the book.

In this respect it must be emphasized that this book is not trying to sell a particular lathe, machine or tool. Although makes and models may be mentioned, and sometimes even described in detail, they are included to show what can be done and what is currently being used; perhaps the inclusion of some will inspire you to go on and make a further development of your own. Many of the top professional turners have produced their own machines and tools, and it is these that have then been taken up by the major manufacturers. Almost every piece of equipment mentioned in this book first reached the market in this way.

So, let's get started! Note that the book does deal with spindle turning from scratch: it begins at the very beginning, just as a student does on the first day of a course. Some more experienced turners may therefore wish to skip the early chapters on spindle-turning basics since they really are just that. However, it is interesting to perceive, when I am demonstrating to a group at a woodturning club, just how often I get asked to go over the elements of using a skew chisel – and I always accede to such requests with great pleasure. One of my greatest joys in turning is to produce long clean lines of smooth skew chisel-finished items; there is even joy to be had in dashing off a quick batch of garden dibbers! And if, some day, when things have gone wrong and stress is beginning to build, I go back into the workshop for a couple of hours in the evening and turn some full-sized eggs (mainly spindle-turned) using the skew, then the stress goes, and I really am restored to a happy equilibrium! Please join me.

—— 2 ——

LONG AND ROUND

Spindles are turned from pieces of wood in which the length is usually many times the width or cross-section, and the grain runs from end to end. The strength of the piece – meaning its resistance to breaking or snapping – will depend upon two things: first the nature of the particular type of wood being used, and secondly the lie of the grain. Almost all woods will split much more easily along the grain than across it, and the reason for this is simple.

THE IMPORTANCE OF GRAIN

Think of a piece of timber as a bunch of long drinking straws stuck together with jelly – because in physical terms at least, this is really all that wood is, the fibres in the wood being the tree's drinking straws. Some trees have big, wide straws; others have fine, even microscopic ones. In different woods the length and thickness of the individual fibres is different: in some they are long, fat and 'fibrous'; in others they are short, fine and barely perceptible. Moreover in some woods the bonding between adjacent fibres is much stronger than in others. Usually, but not always, the denser woods have relatively short, thin fibres which are closer together, and the bonding between them is strong; whereas woods with long, soft fibres have a looser, more pithy, softer bonding. Whatever their nature, if you take any one of the fibres and try to snap it in the middle it will probably bend, but it will not break; and as a bunch, the bending but not the

breaking characteristics of the single fibre will have multiplied by however many fibres there are in the bundle. In fact something of considerable strength will have been produced, and you would find similar characteristics whether the the fibres were hairs, blades of grass, lengths of wire, wood fibres, or whatever.

It is in fact easy to split the fibres apart, because the bond is much weaker than the shearing strength of the fibres. It is for this reason that it is easy to whittle slice or plane a piece of wood *along* the grain, while it is much more difficult to cut it across the grain; in fact to cut *across* the grain of a piece of timber we have to use a saw. Now, the saw's multitude of tiny sharp teeth tear their way through the fibres a few at a time, so it could be said that a saw does not really cut wood – it just tears the two lengths apart!

Many spindles have a load-bearing function so they need to be strong, and in particular they must resist shear-breaking. Spindles are therefore cut from timber which is orientated to provide maximum resistance to snapping or shear-breaking: this means that we make them from timber in which the grain (or fibres) run cleanly along the length of the piece. For instance it is important that in a chair leg the grain runs from end to end, and that it does so clear and true; pieces with any 'wildness' in the grain may look interesting and decorative but they are really useless as chair legs. Moreover, as I shall shortly explain, they are almost equally useless in non-structural decorative spindles because they are extremely difficult to cut cleanly.

Let us now think back to some of our childhood whittling with that first treasured pocket knife. Wasn't it easy to peel off long strips? First the bark, and then long shavings of the wood itself. It required only a little more effort to shave down the end to a point, but the wood still cut cleanly, at least until the knife got too blunt. You very quickly learnt one thing, however, and that was, that if you tried to cut up against a rising slope, the knife, however sharp, would not cut the wood, but dug in and split it away in large splinters. You learnt it, modified what you did, and then just ceased to give it a conscious thought. When you start turning you do have to think consciously about such issues, and keep them to the forefront of your mind at all times.

GRAIN AND THE LATHE

The lathe takes all the effort out of cutting or tearing the wood, whatever the direction you approach the grain. Moreover, it is easy to produce whatever profile you want, and while the lathe is turning it all looks fine. But when you stop the lathe and examine the surface of the wood you will see that whilst some parts are cut cleanly and the

Fig. 6 If the grain in the spindle is not true it is easy to get torn surfaces.

finish is smooth and clean, other parts are torn and the surface is ragged and fluffy; you may also see a series of ridges or ripples. From this it becomes clear that the art of spindle turning lies in ensuring that you are always cutting along the grain and down across the ends of the bunch of fibres, and never across the grain, or up under either the sides or the ends of the fibres.

PLANING WITH A JACK PLANE

Look at what happens when we plane a piece of wood with a jack plane. First we start with a nice plank of knot-free timber and plane it from end to end; the plane is sharp and is set to take just a fine cut. The angle of the edge of the blade is such that it wants to dig into the timber, and as the plane is pushed along the shaving developing on the top of the plane's blade tries to push the blade deeper into the wood. However the shoe of the plane, acting as a bevel rubbing along the top of the timber, prevents the downward thrust from deepening the cut. The blade now travels along the fibres and neatly separates off a small bunch to form a shaving. There is very little resistance and, provided the blade is sharp, we get an even cut with even thickness shavings from end to end of the timber.

Now, still working on the top of the piece of timber, try to plane across the surface at right-angles to the run of the grain: if your plane is razor sharp you *may* just make a clean cut. However, it is more likely that you will tear some splinters off the surface, and there may well also be some small shavings. What has happened is that the tip of the blade has come in against the side of a fibre and has tried to cut through it, but the fibre has just been torn from its bed and has then rolled away from the rest of the bunch; it was easier for it to wrench itself free of the bonding to its next-door neighbour than it was for your blade to slice through its middle from side to side. (Basically it is easier

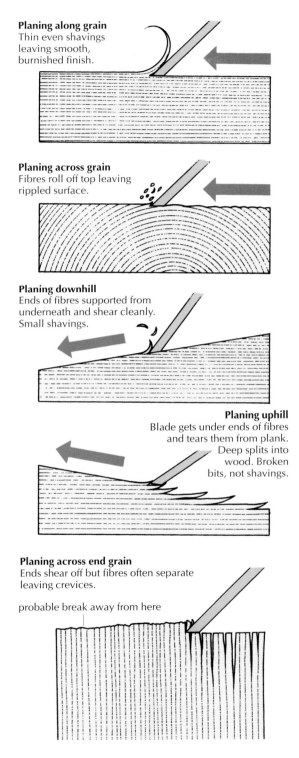

Planing along grain
Thin even shavings leaving smooth, burnished finish.

Planing across grain
Fibres roll off top leaving rippled surface.

Planing downhill
Ends of fibres supported from underneath and shear cleanly. Small shavings.

Planing uphill
Blade gets under ends of fibres and tears them from plank. Deep splits into wood. Broken bits, not shavings.

Planing across end grain
Ends shear off but fibres often separate leaving crevices.

probable break away from here

Fig. 7 Planing along, up, down or across the grain.

for a saw to prise the jelly apart than to cut into the side of the straw.)

CHAMFERING OFF THE TIMBER END

Move to the end of the timber: you are now going to produce a bevel by chamfering off the end. This time you are working along the grain, but by tipping your plane slightly you no longer retain sole contact and you encourage the blade to cut down into the timber. Each cut snips a sloping cut off the ends of the fibres, but because these are bonded down their length to their neighbours, they remain in place: your downward force does not cause them to break off because they are fully supported from underneath by the mass of fibres in the body of the timber below them. So you get a smooth cut with shorter, thicker shavings.

What happens if you turn round and try to plane *up* the slope? This is a whole different story and the absolute opposite of the previous situation. The blade makes its initial entry and a bunch of fibres builds up on top of the edge. It wants to go much deeper but the plane's sole will not let it, and you are already under the ends of fibres. Again they prefer to unbond themselves rather than shear through, so they split away from their neighbours and now there is nothing on top to support them so ultimately they break. The plane judders forwards, takes another bite, digs in, and the next set of fibre-ends break away leaving you with a broken, deep pitted surface. Fibres which are particularly fat and flexible, as in pinewood, do not break off sharply but bend over and do not get cut or break immediately, resulting in a torn surface with little fluffs of wood sticking out of the timber. Torn grain is the bane of every wood turner.

PLANING THE END GRAIN

To complete the picture, re-clamp the timber with the end of the plank or baulk uppermost and plane across this; you are now working across open end grain, that is, the ends of the bunches of fibres.

Again, the plane has to be very sharp to have any effect at all; it also requires a substantial amount of push to move it forwards and to snip the ends off the fibres. All may be well until you get near to the far edge. Now the force required to cut through the fibres exceeds the capability of their bonding matrix to hold them together, so a piece of wood breaks away from the edge. The actual cut surface prior to the final break may also be finely pitted, as a small bunch of fibres may have started to break away from its neighbours, and did so until the body mass prevented it going any further and it sheared.

There is one other lesson to draw from these simple exercises: it may be cause or it may be effect, but the faster the plane blade traverses the wood – as in planing down the length of a piece of smooth grain – then the cleaner is the cut.

TURNING A SPINDLE

Any one of these problems may manifest itself in spindle turning – actually in any form of turning – but if you understand them and think them through, they will teach you all you need to know about choice of tool and angle of tool presentation, and even about lathe speeds. So let's apply the thinking to turning a spindle.

For the moment we will not concern ourselves with the various means of holding wood on the lathe, but will just clamp up a piece to work on using a basic cross-head drive centre and normal revolving tailstock point. These are the basic drive fittings usually supplied with the lathe.

Timber is a valuable resource so we want to waste as little as possible. The first thing that this means is that we always want to mount the wood block or length on the lathe as near as possible to the wood's central axis. For spindle turning we may start with a round section, but usually what we start with is a piece of timber that is square or near square.

There are various methods of locating the exact centre of a square section. The easiest is to draw two diagonal lines each joining the opposite corners, and where the lines cross is the centre. Indent this point as carefully as possible using a centre punch, and then do the same at the other end of the length.

We want to ensure a positive drive, so the drive spur must have a good purchase on the timber: to achieve this it is driven into the end grain of the wood.

ROUGHING THE WOOD TO A ROUND

The first task is to 'rough the wood to a round': this means turning the square-section timber until it is a clean cylinder. For most of us this is a task we normally do with little thought, but there are nevertheless some important aspects of it, and it provides us with a useful platform on which to base our introduction to lathe cutting principles. To detail the process, the wood is going to rotate and every rotation presents the cutting tool with four protruding corners, so initially there will be four clear bangs at every turn; then as the corners get cut away, the noise and the shocks on the turning tool will begin to subside.

THE ROUGHING GOUGE

The tool used is called a roughing gouge: it has to be strong enough to sustain the repeated shocks, and certainly not to break. It also has to be shaped so that there is no risk of the corners of the blade digging in and possibly wrenching the timber off the

(Above) *Fig. 8 Finding the centre by drawing lines joining diagonally opposite corners.*

(Above right) *Fig. 9 Indenting the central turning axis with a centre punch.*

(Right) *Fig. 10 Driving a spur into the centre. A rubber hammer ensures that the morse taper is not damaged.*

lathe mounts. Like all turning tools it has a longer blade than ordinary woodworking chisels; this is so that it can reach the work while the blade itself is firmly supported on the lathe's tool-rest. It is a gouge rather than a simple, flat chisel. This means that the cross-section is a U in form; in fact, in the case of the roughing gouge it is a deep U, rather like the cross-section of a glaciated Norwegian fiord. With this cutting-edge profile it is extremely difficult to catch the corners of the blade on the rotating timber. Not

19

Fig. 11 Roughing gouge in use, with the bevel rubbing and the optimum 45-degree angle of presentation. Note how close the rest is to the timber.

only this, being a deep U means that the edge is in the form of a trough or arc, and so only a small section is in contact with the timber; therefore only a small cut can be made, thus reducing the load on the drive motor, and ensuring that there is no risk of digging in too deep.

Every knob, knot or imperfection on the rotating wood, and particularly the corners of squared section, hits the cutting edge of the tool with a downward movement, and this has a chain of consequence. First, it can cause the tool to bend or flex to a certain degree, and this in turn causes the tip to bounce in and out of cutting contact; as a result a ripple can be created on the timber. Obviously the greater the overhang between the point at which the blade is resting on the tool-rest and the cutting edge, the greater will be the amplitude of the bounce. Also the greater the overhang, the more downward force is exerted on the cutting edge, and the more leverage on the handle, so the right hand tends to be knocked up. This in turn can also cause the edge to bite deeper into the wood.

Fortunately the design of the roughing gouge blade – big, solid, and with a deep U – provides a structure that does not flex. With shallow Us, and flat chisel-bladed tools in particular, flexing can become a major problem. We will talk a lot more about this a little later on.

Reducing Bouncing
Bouncing is a problem when roughing, and there are two techniques that arise from this. First – and this applies to all stages in spindle turning – it is important to keep the amount of blade overhang to the very minimum, which means keeping the tool-rest as close as possible to the wood. When we start roughing, the rest is set so that it lies on or just under the axis of the piece on the lathe (just about level with the lateral centre of the timber) and about ⅛in (3mm) clear of the rotating corners. Obviously as we start turning, the corners are quickly cut away and the gap widens. Stop the lathe every so often and reset the rest closer to the wood to reduce the gap.

Bouncing and vibration is also reduced by holding the tool's blade firmly and pressing it down onto the tool rest. 'Firmly' for roughing means a positive grip, although certainly not to the extent of having white knuckles; and as the cylinder becomes smoother, the grip softens. When you get to cutting fine detail, a couple of fingers resting lightly on top of the blade is 'firm' enough.

BASIC PRINCIPLES

Fundamental to every cut you ever make in turning there is one absolute principle. Think back to the jack plane. You never start a plane cut with the blade already resting on the zone you are cutting: you *always* start with the shoe of the plane resting on the wood and then you advance the plane until the blade starts to cut; you then carry on to complete the cutting stroke. Turning tools are used in the same way. The bevel behind the cutting edge is your plane's sole – you always start with this resting on the area you wish to cut and then you slowly draw the blade back towards you until the edge starts to cut, and the edge is now supported by the bevel rubbing just in front (the rotating wood is coming towards you) of where the actual cut is occurring. It is this that controls the depth and smoothness of the cut.

So, rule number one is to start with the bevel rubbing, and *never* to go straight into the wood with the cutting edge. Every time you break this rule the edge will dig in and will spoil the cut.

ROUGHING TECHNIQUE

So, the wood blank is on the lathe. Set the lathe speed to between 750 and 1,000rpm. With the roughing gouge, the back of the blade rests on the tool-rest and the bevel on the top of the rotating timber. When you start with a square section this causes a little bouncing and makes a noise like an old outboard engine.

The blade is drawn back until chippings start to fly. Moving the blade sideways along the tool-rest takes off the worst of the corners on the wood. At this stage the tool is held with the axis of the blade at a slight angle to the axis of the timber. The blade points in the direction you are cutting, so it leads the handle by 10 or so degrees to the left while making a left sweep. The right hand is holding the handle just behind the widest zone (3in (76mm) or so back from the ferrule). A good position for the left hand is with the fingers wrapped round over the top of the blade with your thumb towards you. The U is canted over a little to the left – probably 5 to 10 degrees off the upright, so the cut is occurring just a little to the right of the trough of the U.

When making the sweep, take care that you don't fall off the end of the tool-rest.

Now cut back the other way, from left to right. If you must you can change hands; and you really do need to become fully ambidextrous and use either right or left hand to cut in both directions. For this simple roughing activity however, try not to change hands. Roll the tool to lean the U over to the right, bring the right hand across the tummy to the left and let the cutting edge again lead the tool this time to the right. Sweep back and forth in a continuous motion until the sound of the cutting has softened from a machine-gun rattle to a gentle swish.

THE THUMB TEST

The wood should now be close to a clean cylinder, and you can test it without stopping the lathe: hold your hand above the rotating timber with your thumb pointing towards you, and let the thumb touch lightly on the top of the wood. If you feel any unevenness, you are not quite there and another couple of passes might be required. If, on the other hand the cylinder feels smooth, stop the lathe and check.

The tool-rest or rests that you have are unlikely to be of sufficient length that you

Fig. 12 The thumb test; any unevenness is readily felt.

can work the complete length of the timber without frequently repositioning the post and rest. We will talk more about tool-rests in the chapter on lathes and equipment, but for the moment just accept that the tool-rest carriage may have to be repositioned several times down the length of the lathe bed in order to reduce the whole length of the timber to a cylinder.

Roughing gouges are designed to do rough things to rough wood, so we do tend to use them aggressively and with little attention to the niceties of tool presentation (except for always starting with the bevel rubbing). As you pick up the next tool, however, a skew chisel, we jump to the other end of the scale.

THE SKEW CHISEL

A round cylinder is brought to a finished smoothness with a skew chisel. The skew is the wood turner's jack plane, but it is also used to produce long tapers (as a plane might), and as we will see later, it may be used for rounding over (as would a spoke

shave) and even for turning beads. It is like a carpenter's chisel except that it has a double bevel on the cutting edge so that it may be used either way up; and the edge is always at an angle to the axis of the blade. Let us consider why it is shaped like this – and to do so, we need to go back to our earlier thoughts about planing.

We saw that it was easy to plane down a length following the grain of the wood, whereas planing across the plank caused splinters to be pulled from the surface. In a spindle blank mounted on a lathe the grain lies along the the axis of the lathe, but the wood is spinning around its own axis. If we tried to plane straight down the length with the cutting edge of the tool at right-angles to the axis, the wood would merely revolve under the edge of the tool and we would certainly not cut anything away. And if we tried to plane across the rotating timber (across the grain) we would see exactly the same results as we would in jack planing across a board: that is we would remove splinters and leave long tears down the wood. Therefore neither 0 degrees to the axis, nor 90 degrees to it are any good, and

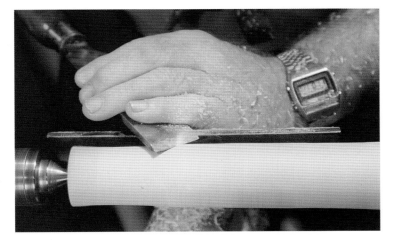

Fig. 13 (Right) Skew planing with the bevel rubbing, 45-degree edge presentation, and steadying fingers resting lightly on the blade.
(Below) Skew pass in the reverse direction.

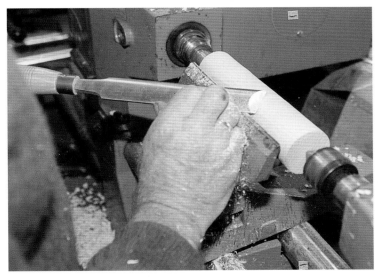

so we compromise at a nice, efficient 45 degrees whereby the blade of the skew planes down the length of the cylinder at an angle of 45 degrees to the axis.

Ideally if we swept the skew chisel sideways at a sufficiently fast rate with an edge presentation angle of 45 degrees, and with the lathe turning at an appropriate speed, we would effectively be planing straight down the same lengths of fibre. Unfortunately, however, we cannot move that fast. But as you think about this idea, it does raise another issue: if you were trying to take a cut along the length of a piece of static timber with a carpenter's bevel chisel, how sharp would the edge have to be? Now think how blunt, relatively speaking, are the turning tools we so often use, and consider that perhaps some of the poor finishes we see on turned wood would disappear if we took more care over the sharpening of turning tools.

To return to our 45 degree angle: if we used an ordinary flat chisel with the usual 90 degree, edge-to-blade angle, we would have to hold the handle way out to the side in order to achieve a 45-degree-to-axis presentation. This would be awkward at best, but it would also be much more difficult to hold steady and to control the tool, and it may even at times foul against some part of the lathe. By having an angled edge we can achieve a 45-degree, edge-presentation angle with the handle of the tool held somewhere close in to the waist – in its most controllable position.

ARC SKEWS

Most professional turners now use skews where the edge is ground not at a single angle to the blade, but to an arc, curve or semi-circle. This gives huge advantages. First, in most skew work the cut is made in the middle of the cutting edge. If you get near to a corner, there is a chance of it slipping and digging in deeply, totally ruining the work (and giving the turner heart failure!). Moreover, the two ends of the blade's tip are always perilously close to catching; some teachers of turning put red paint on the two ends of the skew's cutting edge to show where the 'no go' zones are. (Of course you cannot keep the points painted or covered as we actually use these in later cuts.)

By having a ground edge in the shape of an arc we achieve two things: first it places the two ends much further back from the working zone, and the danger of 'dig-in; is greatly reduced. Second, while the centre of the arc may provide a 45-degree contact angle with the tool held near to the turner's waist, we may move the cut along the edge thereby changing the presentation angle; or alternatively, move the hand away from, or across the waist and still achieve the desired 45 degrees.

THE IDEAL SKEW POSITION

Modern skews have also developed in another way. If you have ever tried jack planing where you could not work flat on the top of the plank, but had to work on some sloping or rounded face, you will know how difficult it is to maintain an even angle of bevel. So when, in turning, we are planing with a skew chisel, we work on top of the rotating timber. This means that the bevel of the tool is on top, and the blade can lie flat on the tool-rest with the top of the rest only a fraction below the height of the top of the timber.

Obviously a flat blade rests nicely on a flat (horizontal) tool-rest. A few moments ago, however, we mentioned that skews can be used for planing down tapered section and even for rounding over beads and suchlike. This means that while the blade may start flat, it is going to have to be rolled onto its side as the cutting edge moves from the horizontal towards the vertical. To accommodate this the best skews today have curved cutting edges and are oval in section, with no sharp corners to the short point side of the blade.

The last basic point before we start skew planing is to ensure that the top edge of the tool-rest is smooth. They are often

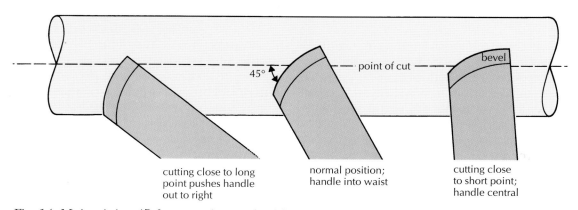

45°

point of cut

bevel

cutting close to long
point pushes handle
out to right

normal position;
handle into waist

cutting close
to short point;
handle central

Fig. 14 Maintaining 45-degree cutting angle with arc-ground skew.

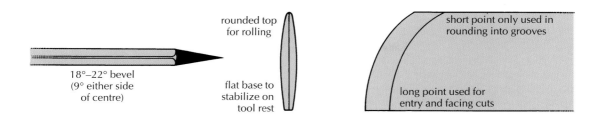

18°–22° bevel
(9° either side
of centre)

rounded top
for rolling

flat base to
stabilize on
tool rest

short point only used in
rounding into grooves

long point used for
entry and facing cuts

Fig. 15 Section through oval skew. Note it is flat on long point side for vertical cutting.

made of cast iron or soft steel and can get bruised, marked or notched. If there are imperfections, the edge of a square-cornered skew can catch and break the flow of a sweep. If there are any marks on a tool-rest, dress the rest with a file to get a smooth, nicely rounded running track.

The basic skewing position also means having the tool rest right up, often at its maximum height. We also said earlier that we wanted the minimum overhang, and this may mean positioning the tool-post close to the spindle so that the edge of the rest is sticking out over the timber itself.

SKEW PLANING TECHNIQUE

Skew planing is a gentle process. If done properly, with long sweeping cuts, 45-degree presentation, nice high lathe speed (more on speeds later), with the tool held with TLC (tender loving care), and the bevel kept rubbing – then you can produce a burnished finish to the timber that will be far smoother than you can ever achieve in any other way, even with the finest grade of abrasives. This should be your target, and it is worth practising on waste timber until you can achieve such a quality of finish.

So set the lathe speed up to about double the speed you used for roughing. On a 1 to 2in (25 to 50mm) diameter spindle

you should now be at around 1,500rpm, although later, when you are more skilled, you may choose to work at double this speed. Basically, the faster the speed of rotation the smoother the finish; *but*! the faster the speed, the easier it is for a novice to make mistakes (and all in a lightning flash). The speed and the sound can also be quite frightening. (The professionals turn ⅜in (9mm) diameter lace bobbins at speeds of around 10,000rpm.)

STANCE

Stance is important for many reasons. First for comfort, you want to aim for an even bodyweight distribution on your hips, knees and feet if you are going to spend all day at the lathe. Then there is the matter of control. Every time you twist the body at the waist you alter the plane in which the tool is sweeping – moving the feet in the middle of a cut is worse. You should aim to make continuous sweeps from one end of the spindle to the other, and to do this without too much twisting at the waist or changing the position of the feet at all. An ideal stance for most turners is with the feet apart and the left foot just in advance of the right (this allows you to swing backwards and forwards); and have the front of the torso parallel to the lathe's axis, because there is then no need to twist. The elbows rest on the waist and the forearms are parallel with the floor.

25

HOLDING TECHNIQUE

The more delicate the work, the less leverage you need on the tool handle and the more accurate the control that you want. This is always achieved by holding the handle of the tool nearer the front. My preference is to hold the handle of the skew around the widest part only an inch or two from the ferrule. For most planing the steadying hand is used by placing only two or three fingers on the top of the blade; these can control and dampen out any vibration tendency, without applying any real pressure.

For a right-handed person, the first sweep is probably from the outboard end in towards the left, so the handle is in the right hand and the first three fingers of the left hand are used to steady. If you are planing a parallel-walled cylinder, you can make each successive cut in the same direction (and vice versa for the left-handed). However few turning jobs have parallel-walled cylinders – and remember you can only plane 'downhill' (working down the ends of supported grain). So even when working parallel walls it is best to plane first in one direction, and then back in the other, and so on.

When roughing we merely changed the angle of the tool, but did not change hands. In skewing you have to change hands – you cannot just change the angle of presentation by doing a cross-hands boogie! You must become ambidextrous! So now change hands and plane back in the opposite direction.

PRODUCING A TAPER

Most short courses start with the student making a handle for a turning tool, and this really is an ideal exercise. On a turning tool there is usually a grip just inboard of the blade: this is the widest section. Between this and the blade there is a rounded-over end, and then a reduced parallel section into which the blade tang is driven and on which there is a strengthening ferrule. Further down the handle it tapers down to a narrow waist, and then it tapers back out again to a wider section at the heel. This wide section is sometimes held when we are doing heavy work (roughing really wild pieces for a big bowl) and you need maximum leverage and shock absorbency. It also provides a counter-balance to the weight of the blade.

Clearly, if you are to avoid uphill turning (coming up under the ends of unsupported grain and getting considerable tearing) you have to cut down one side of the waist taper to the lowest point, and then change hands and come down the other side of the taper, again to the lowest point.

SUMMARY

So now we have turned our piece of wood into a round with a roughing gouge; we have smoothed the cylinder with a skew chisel, and have then produced a taper. It may be a continuous taper all in one direction, or a compound taper where the diameter at both ends is reduced in to provide a narrower waist. The taper could be 'flat' – that is, the diameter constantly reducing at the same rate – or it could be slightly curved to provide a concave or convex profile. After roughing, the work is all done with a skew held delicately on the top of the tool-rest, and the rest is nearly level with the top of the rotating wood.

In the next chapter we will consider the full range of cuts used in spindle turning, and how they fit together to build up decorative features.

— 3 —

THE CUTS

Decoration on spindles falls into two broad categories: the first is circular in form and is lathe-applied; the second is spiral or longitudinal and is hand- or router-cut. In this chapter we are going to look at all the basic shapes used in circular decoration, and at the tools and techniques used to produce them. On some spindles there may be only one or two features, on others there may be a whole string, often with repeats. Here we are going to make no judgements about design or aesthetics, nor about the structural implications of putting some features side by side; for the moment our only concern is with how to make the shapes.

Let us begin by looking at the full range of basic spindle turning shapes you may wish to produce at some time or another. For illustration we will simply string them out on one spindle – a totally unusual spindle that nobody in their right mind would ever make other than for practice! We will also give each profile its proper name – as far as anyone has ever agreed a 'proper' name!

Our piece starts with a typical feature encountered on most chair or table legs: it has a squared section into which frame and cross-members are mortised. This then becomes the round of our decorated part, and the turning of the square-to-round junction does require particular skills. Next we go immediately into a bead, and this ends in the first of our fillets. A fillet is a short parallel section and is put before and/or after a feature to give the feature definition. As a point of design interest, running a string of features together with-

Fig. 16 Basic spindle-turning shapes.

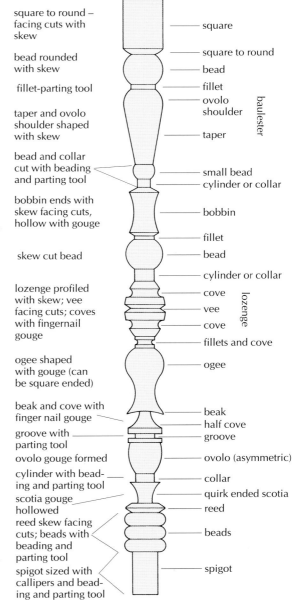

square to round – facing cuts with skew

bead rounded with skew

fillet-parting tool

taper and ovolo shoulder shaped with skew

bead and collar cut with beading and parting tool

bobbin ends with skew facing cuts, hollow with gouge

skew cut bead

lozenge profiled with skew; vee facing cuts; coves with fingernail gouge

ogee shaped with gouge (can be square ended)

beak and cove with finger nail gouge

groove with parting tool

ovolo gouge formed

cylinder with beading and parting tool

scotia gouge hollowed

reed skew facing cuts; beads with beading and parting tool

spigot sized with callipers and beading and parting tool

square

square to round

bead

fillet

ovolo shoulder

taper

baulester

small bead

cylinder or collar

bobbin

fillet

bead

cylinder or collar

cove

vee

cove

lozenge

fillets and cove

ogee

beak

half cove

groove

ovolo (asymmetric)

collar

quirk ended scotia

reed

beads

spigot

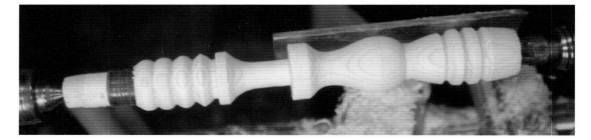

Fig. 17 Some basic shapes. From the left: a spigot with metal ferrule; a row of beads with final reed; a quirk; a scotia; a facing cut; and a lozenge with grooves (two cove and one vee).

out an occasional fillet to break them up makes the piece look cluttered.

There is then a long taper which starts with a rounded-over shoulder technically known as an 'ovolo'. The straight taper terminates in a small bead, followed by a short parallel section or cylinder, which is too long to be a fillet. The next feature is known as a 'bobbin', with an inclined, usually straight, shoulder at each end; then comes a symmetrical concave joining the two peaks. After another fillet, a good, solid larger bead comes next, followed by a small collar.

Now we come to a complex group with secondary decoration cut into a feature. The basic form is of a convex lozenge or 'sausage'. In some texts you may see these erroneously called 'bobbins'. Into the top of the lozenge we have two standard but small, semi-circular coves separated by a small 'vee' groove or notch. Vee grooves are sometimes called 'quirks', but the name is correctly applied to a separating feature which has a vertical face and really brings a feature to an end. Again the word 'quirk' is sometimes misused, some turners applying the name to what we here call fillets (and in the past I have done it myself). The true definitions of 'fillet' and 'quirk' come from classical architecture where they were used to describe features on

columns. A true quirk can be seen at each end of the ogee, which is a little further along the spindle.

The lozenge ends with a small cove (with two defining tiny fillets), which separates it from the compound curve feature which starts with a rounded-over shoulder (ovolo) and then goes through a concave waisted section. This compound has a profile known as an 'ogee'. The fillet ends this feature and separates it from what in classical architecture is called a 'beak'. Beyond the beak we have a semi-circular cove. A straight-walled groove is cut into a short cylinder, and then there is an asymmetrical ovolo. A scotia (an asymmetrical cove) follows, with a quirk at each end. This ends in a pyramid-form reed, and a row of small beads. However, we will be going a little further on this useless demonstration piece, because to the outboard of the beads there is a waste zone. This is sized down to a spigot onto which a copper ferrule is fitted, as we would put on a tool handle.

Obviously, for exercise you can cut any of these elements to whatever size you wish. You could *try* to cut them onto a single long spindle, although if you did, you would get all sorts of flexing and vibration problems; so you will find it easier to cut just two or three features on short test pieces. What matters for the moment is their shapes and tooling, not the size or sequence.

THE SEVEN BASIC CUTS

Let us take a hard look at this spindle of many shapes, because most of the elements repeat and we can actually reduce all the profiles shown to a few basic cutting/turning processes.

First, as detailed earlier, we have the **roughing** process, and then the smoothing into a long parallel-wall cylinder by **planing** with a skew. Skew planing is also the process used to produce long tapers, both straight-walled and slightly convex. There are also a number of places where a whole but short or mini-cylinder are required; this includes the fillets. They differ from long cylinders in that often you cannot get in with a skew, as adjacent features interfere with access. You use either a parting tool (for small fillets) or a beading and parting tool (for short cylinders). Many of these features also serve as

sizing elements, and they can all be regarded as sizing cuts.

There are then many points at which a **rounding-over** is required. This can be a short-radius rounding, as in the ovolo at the start of the long taper, and in all of the beads; or a longer radius as on the lozenge, the inboard end of the ogee and the asymmetrical ovolo. For all rounding-over cuts we use some form of skew; only for the very tightest of radii, as in the small beads, do we use the beading and parting tool. Again with the exception of the small beads we could also use a shallow U-gouge, usually with a 'finger nail' profile.

The next basic set of shapes comprises the variety of concave areas, essentially all '**scoopings out**'. There are long-radius curves on the bobbin and the second part of the ogee; the half coves following the beak and that of the scotia; and the tighter radius, small half-circle coves cut into the lozenge. All these are scooping cuts made with shallow U-gouges. The edge may be finger nail or almost square in profile.

We have only one example of a **hollowing out** cut: this is the undercutting under the beak. Much deeper hollowing cuts are used to produce goblet bowls and for this a small, deep, U-bowl gouge is normally used.

The final group consists of **vertical or facing cuts**, done with a skew held on its side, although there are times when a shallow U-gouge might also be considered. Facing cuts are to be found in the square-to-round junction; at the end of the cylinder preceding the asymmetrical ovolo; and again

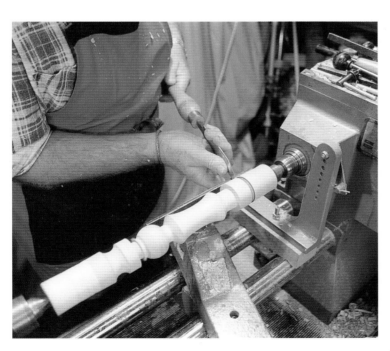

Fig. 18 More basic shapes. From the left: cove; fillet; large bead; fillet; bobbin; cylinder; and start of large bead.

preceding the fillet just before the scotia. The sloping shoulders of the reed may be treated in this way, and the shoulders of the bobbin might be made as facing cuts.

And there you have it, the whole of spindle turning reduced to seven cuts: roughing, planing, rounding-over, scooping, hollowing out, facing, and finally sizing. Basically this means developing skills with, at most, six types of tool. You will probably build up an armoury of different sizes of tool, each with some slight difference in edge profile, and you will have both a thin parting and a broader beading and parting tool, but basically there are only six types. Some of the great old time-served turners reduced it to even less than that and used just an all-purpose gouge, a skew, and a parter!

So let's look at each of these seven skill areas in turn. In fact, we have already covered the basics of roughing and skew planing so these sections are largely by way of resumé.

THE ROUGHING CUT

Roughing starts with the lathe set to a lower speed. For a 2–3in (50–76mm) square blank this will mean about 750rpm (depending on the speeds you have available). The tool-rest is set at the axis height. It is positioned as close as possible to the outermost corner of the timber, and the timber is hand-rotated to check clearance before the lathe is switched on.

The roughing gouge has a deep U-profile and is of rugged construction to withstand shock loading. We use large tools; how large will be determined by the main stream of your work, but blades of 1½ and 2in (38 and 50mm) width are not uncommon. Obviously if you only ever turn lace bobbins you probably would not bother to have a special roughing tool.

It is held firmly in your natural hand (usually the right), with a grip somewhere on the waist just behind the wide zone. The left or steadying hand is over the top of the blade with the fingers curled round underneath. The heel of the tool is tucked into the side of the waist. The stance is with the trunk square to the lathe's axis, feet slightly apart and the left foot leading.

The tool is placed with the middle of the back of the blade on the top of the tool-rest, with the outer end of the blade back resting on top of the rotating timber; the tool is therefore inclined upwards. It is also angled slightly so that the cutting edge is pointing in the direction you will be cutting. The U is canted over by 5 or so degrees. It will be bouncing as each revolving corner strikes it.

In fact, the roughing gouge may be used at right-angles to the lathe's axis and the U upright; this can give the lightest cut. From here, the tool may be angled to up to the 45 degrees used with the skew, and the U may be upright or canted over by 5 or so degrees; this usually gives the heaviest cut.

Draw the blade back until first the bevel rubs on the timber; then it starts cutting. Do not draw it any further back, but now start to slide the tool along the rest to cut along the length. When you reach the end of the timber, push the tool forwards slightly so that the blade back now rests on the timber. Swing the heel of the tool across the front of your stomach so that the blade is now angled to point back along the timber in the new direction of travel. Draw the blade back until the bevel rubs and then cut.

Continue to sweep backwards and forwards until you no longer feel the bounce of corners hitting the chisel and there is the swishing sound of a smooth and even cut. Do the thumb test; you will feel any unevenness if you have not quite got a round. If it feels right, stop the lathe and look.

Two points should be made here: first, as the corners are cut away, the gap between wood and tool-rest will widen, and in your early days of turning it is advisable to stop the lathe and reposition the rest closer. As you become more experienced and the need for output pushes you towards short cuts, then you may not stop the lathe to reposition the rest, or you may not even bother to reposition until you move on to the next stage of planing. The second point is that you can always rough smaller diameter spindles with the skew, but there is a risk that this sometimes tears large splinters off the wood and this may wreck your workpiece.

SKEW-PLANING CUTS

As we saw earlier, the essence of skew planing is to maintain a cutting angle of about 45 degrees between the tool edge and the axis of the spindle. The cut is also made with the edge on the top of the cylinder. This means having the tool-rest right up, often near the top of its travel. In order to keep the overhang of the tool blade to the minimum, the rest is brought as close as possible to the cylinder. The speed of the lathe is increased so that a 2in (50mm) diameter spindle is spun at 1,500rpm (you may later raise this to 2,000 or 2,500rpm).

The skew must be kept sharp and is held lightly in the natural hand. The grip is probably around the widest part of the handle, and you will see many turners planing with the right index finger lying along the top of the blade. The steadying hand merely guides the cut with two or three fingers resting lightly on the top of the blade.

As with the roughing gouge, and indeed all cutting tools, the cut is started with the blade back lying across both the tool-rest and the top of the timber. It is then drawn back until the bevel rubs and cutting starts.

While the optimum cut is achieved with an angle of 45 degrees between cutting edge and spindle axis, the tool will in fact cut over a wide range of angles. Shallower angles are more likely to make big cuts, but they are also much more likely to take off splinters.

Steeper angles (50 degrees and upwards) cut more slowly. At all times you must avoid pushing the skew downwards onto the cylinder, as this is likely to cause flexing and vibration. Should you get flexing, a small wave will form on the surface and this will rapidly get deeper. To get rid of it, reduce the pressure and increase the angle of attack.

Long tapers, long convex curve slopes, and even very shallow concave areas can be cut with the skew. But remember the golden rule, always to cut 'downhill': that is, from the greater diameter to the lesser

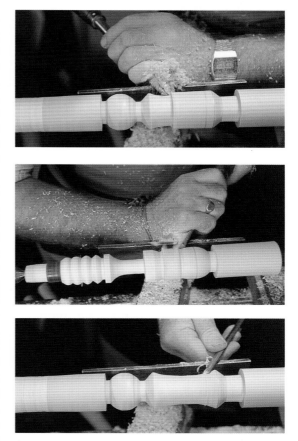

Fig. 19 Cutting downhill into the low point of a bobbin (top); here a square-ended gouge is being used (middle); the final cut with a shallow gouge (bottom).

31

so you are working over the ends of supported fibres; this means that on curved features, concave or convex, you work down one side and then down the other, and never continuously along the whole length of the feature (down and then up).

In terms of choice of skew, the case has already been made for the oval section with a curved cutting edge; this will be further emphasized in a few minutes when we come to rounding-over. One thing to be avoided is the use of big, old-fashioned, square-sectioned skews with ⅜in (10mm) thick blades; they are massive and unwieldy, and no wonder turners are afraid of them!

There are some poor turners who never come to terms with the skew and they only ever use a shallow U-gouge. The gouge is easier because it is less likely to catch, but it never gives you the burnish nor the crisp corners that you can achieve with a properly handled skew.

ROUNDING OVER

Often at the top end of a long sweeping taper there is a rounded shoulder, and these are also best cut with a skew. It is here that the modern oval-section skews really come into their own.

CUTTING A ROUNDED SHOULDER

Take a look at the long taper near the head of our funny spindle: you have cut the fillet to its finished diameter and planed down the taper, and you now have a short cylinder between the fillet and the beginning of the slope of the taper.

To roll the shoulder, start with the tool-rest at a little above the height of the bottom of the groove of the fillet; this will put it a few millimetres below the normal planing position.

If you now hold the skew on the top of the cylinder, as for planing, it will be clearly

Fig. 20 Rounding over with an arc-ground skew.

angled upwards with the handle below the top of the tool-rest. The skew is held with the back of the blade flat on the rest. The first cut starts with the cutting zone right in the middle of the tool's edge, and with the edge at the ideal 45 degrees to the cylinder's axis. The cut starts about ⅕in (5mm) in from the edge of the groove. Draw back the blade through the bevel contact until the cut starts. As the blade moves towards the edge of the groove, roll the tool so that the outboard side of the blade lifts off the tool-rest; at the same time start to lift the handle slightly. This will cut off the corner at the top of the groove. Go back and make a second similar cut. On the third cut you may start another millimetre from the edge, and this time try to maintain cutting to well down the inside wall of the groove. Eventually you reach the stage where the blade starts flat on the tool-rest, but ends vertically deep in the groove. The handle will also have risen well above the rest in order to drive the cutting edge right down to the bottom of the groove. You will find that the right hand lifts and sweeps out-wards and up, tracing a semicircular arc.

Your right elbow will also have swung up until it is right out to the side and level with the shoulder. The sequence of similar cuts continues until you have a nice rounded over shoulder with an even curve from the point of maximum diameter down to the base of the groove.

In your early days expect two problems. Sometimes the cut will have moved along the tool's edge until it is too close to the short point, which then catches on the face of the shoulder; the tool is pushed back up the face and you have accidentally cut a spiral groove. The other potential problem is that you may make a wrong entry and take the apex of the shoulder, producing a mini-flat on the face. Practise, watching the tool edge and the position of the cut very carefully: it *will* come right!.

Rounding-over cuts require a firm grip on the tool handle; the fingers of the left hand are wrapped around the blade.

CUTTING AN EGG SHAPE

To practise the rounding-over technique, take a piece of 2in (50 mm) square timber – 3½in (90mm) plus in length) – and make a wooden egg, working to dimensions you take from a hen's egg with your callipers. Have the point of the egg to the outboard end, and work this until it is almost parted but with about ¼in (5mm) left. Then shape the inboard end again until you have about 5mm left. Finally finish off the outboard end with facing cuts (see below) until you part right through (catch it as it flies!). Cut the rounded end from the disc of drive tim-ber with a sharp knife, and hand sand it to a good curve.

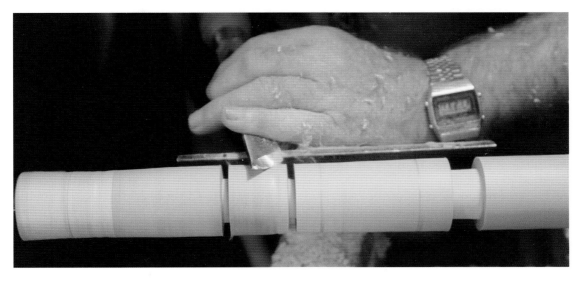

Fig. 21 Rounding a bead with a skew. Note the heel of the hand firmly on the rest.

CUTTING A BEAD

Fundamentally a bead is two 'rounding-overs', one each side of the bead's point of maximum circumference. However, there are two things to watch: first, always keep the cut in the centre of the working zone of the cutting edge, even when the blade has been rolled over to the vertical as the edge plumbs the depths of the groove. Second, you have to be particularly careful about the entry when the bead is near finished: you are starting a planing cut on the apex of a double convex slope, and it is very easy to take too deep a cut and produce a flat topped bead. To avoid this make sure the blade of the skew is flat on the rest and at 45 degrees at least; sometimes for extra safety the angle may be widened a little to 50–55 degrees until the cut is under way. Have the bevel clearly rubbing, and then ease the blade back very slightly to commence the cut. As soon as the cut starts, begin to roll the skew and adjust the cutting angle.

The skew is a chisel with an angle- or arc-profiled cutting edge; the beading and parting tool is also a chisel and it also has a double bevel (both sides of the blade); but the difference is that the 'B & P' is usually narrower in width and much thicker, and the cutting edge is at right-angles to the blade's axis. The standard size is a square-section blade of ⅜in (10mm). These features give it special uses. We earlier touched on its capabilities as a wide parting tool, and as a tool for rapidly reducing the diameter of a cylinder, but it is also particularly useful as a skew for rolling small beads because its rigidity means that the blade cannot flex. Because of this and the narrow overall width of the cutting edge, you can hold it firmly and dig the corner in at an angle without the tool spiralling away along the cylinder. This allows you to take the corner shoulders off a groove very quickly, without going through the multi-pass, small-bit-at-a-time process of rounding over that you do with a skew.

When doing very fine beading work as on a lace bobbin, the beading and parting tool may be too big. Under such circumstances tiny beads can be cut using the much narrower ordinary parting tool.

USING U-GOUGES

Broader-bladed, shallow U-gouges with the edge curved in a fingernail profile, may also be used for rounding over, particularly when making beads. The more nervous turners who suffered a dig-in the early days of their use of a skew tend to favour the gouge! This is understandable: if the arc-ground skew has the corners well back from any danger of catching, then those on the fingernail gouge are practically out of sight! Furthermore, the U-form of the blade means that only the very smallest section of the blade and bevel can be in contact with the wood; thus you just cannot take a big swathe, and it is impossible to accidentally take anything but the smallest and easily reworkable flat off the top of the bead.

Spindle gouges are skew chisels with the corners bent up! They may look very different, as they have only a single bevel (because you can only use them one way up). In some, the cutting edge is 'square' and is at right-angles to the axis of the blade, as in a beading and parting tool; in others it is rounded like a nicely manicured fingernail – here it is, in effect, two arc-ground skews side by side. In a skew the tool can be used either way up, hence the need for two bevels and only a single, semi-circular cutting edge; by turning it over you can cut in either direction. The U-form of the gouge means that it can only be used one way up, so we need the full elongated semicircle for left- and right-hand cuts. But for all this, it really is useful to regard a gouge as a skew chisel with the edges bent up to keep them out of the way! Both types of tool cut in the same way and make modified versions of the same cuts: thus you can plane a parallel cylinder with a shallow U-gouge, and you do have even less chance of a corner catching or dig in.

So why don't we all use them, all of the time? First, without the flat width of the skew blade, the gouge cannot lie flat on the tool-rest in quite the same way, and so a planing cut is not so easy to control; true 'flatness' is therefore more difficult to achieve. Second, you cannot roll a gouge down into a tight groove, and if you try, you will catch its top on the far side of the groove and will produce a major defect. Third, although bevel contact is retained, the rubbing area is minuscule and you don't get the burnishing that the skew will give. Finally, gouges do not have the control and delicacy that is possible with a skew. The gouge may be safer to start with, but you are best advised to learn to do planing and rounding-over properly with a skew.

Before considering the gouge in its role as a scooper, we have yet another important function of the skew to examine.

FACING CUTS

You may find that in rounding deep into a groove, you cannot get right down before your skew starts to bind in the narrow gap. You could now use another skew cut, known as the vertical facing cut, to remove wood from the waste side. This produces vertical or slightly rounded shoulders to a feature; it may also be used to produce 'vee' grooves.

For the facing cut, the tool-rest is set a fraction below the lathe's axis. The skew is laid on the tool-rest with the blade on its side, the long point downwards, and the tool held horizontally (parallel to the ground). In essence, you push the tool straight into the rotating wood with a firm grip – in essence!

There is clearly no bevel rub to control the cut, and if the edge is not vertical and absolutely square to the face of the cylinder,

the tool can kick sideways leaving a spiral groove in the surface. It is therefore advisable to adopt a belt-and-braces grip that limits sideways kick. This requires that the left hand holds the blade from underneath; the forefinger hooks under the tool-rest and the thumb pinches the blade and the rest against the pressure of the forefinger. The main body of the blade is then clamped between the other three fingers and the heel of the hand.

The first cut will not go deep – it cannot, because the resistance of the timber will not allow much penetration – and the depth has to be increased by cutting away the shoulders of the first groove. In the case of a vee cut, this means working one corner and then the other. If, however, it is a vertical face that is being produced, the opposite shoulder has to be worked away to allow tool access.

After the entry cut has been made, all subsequent cuts are bevel-rubbing cuts, and this means angling the skew blade in two planes. Let's say you are cutting the left face: then the skew handle will be slightly out to the right so that the left bevel rubs against the vertical face. It also has to be canted over by 1 to 2 degrees so that the top-side of the blade leans slightly to the right and is just clear of the cut face.

A true, full facing cut will be at right angles to the axis of the spindle. The bevel rubs on the cut face, so if your skew is ground to an overall bevel of, say, 25 degrees, the blade will lie at 12.5 degrees to the cut face. As noted above, it is also leaning over slightly from the face (by 1 or 2 degrees) so that only the bevel down by the long point is in full contact. With an accurate entry it is possible to cut off a paper-thin disc.

This cut is probably the most difficult of all and, at first sight, the precision required looks scary. It is, however, extremely useful, so practice in developing yours skill in facing cuts is very worthwhile. This becomes even

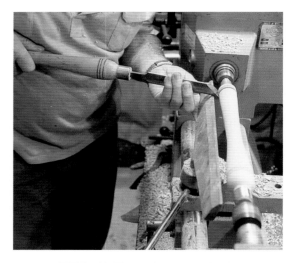

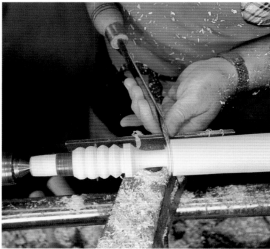

Fig. 22 (Top) Grip for a facing cut with the skew. The index finger pinches the blade onto the rest to prevent sideways kick.
(Bottom) During the development of facing cuts, the lower corner of the bevel is kept rubbing (hence the angle of the handle) and the blade leans 2 degrees from the face.

more apparent when we consider scooping out, because the cutting of tight radius coves with a gouge starts in a very similar manner to commencing a facing cut with a skew.

SCOOPING-OUT CUTS

The ultimate level of short-radius concaves is the semicircular, symmetrical cove, and it is this profile that brings us to the scooping-out cuts. Several gouge cuts start as micro facing cuts, and the semicircular cove is a good example. For these, the tool-rest is set low, just below the lathe's axis height. The gouge makes its initial entry by being pushed into the rotating wood in skew facing-cut position. The blade is held on its side (the centre of the cutting edge being truly vertical), and it is pinch-clamped to the tool-rest so that sideways kicks are resisted. The entry is at right-angles to the surface of the cylinder.

If the edge is not vertical, or if there is a deviation from the right-angles to the surface, the cut will be skewed sideways causing a nasty spiral groove; the tool-rest being too high is one of the first causes of such problems. Almost immediately, however, the cut ceases to be a facing cut, and becomes a 'scooping out'. The tool handle is pushed forwards towards the wood, but at the same time its butt is lowered and the blade is rotated. The cut finishes at the bottom of the groove, by which time a full quarter-turn has been achieved and the edge has risen. The cut runs out with the bevel rubbing flat on the bottom of the groove. The full cove is completed by now making a facing cut entry on the other side, and again scooping towards the bottom of the cove.

Cutting coves is the classic model of cutting downhill: provided you remember this and can make a clean facing-cut entry you know all you need to know about scooping out!

HOLLOWING OUT

There are two basic cuts left. One of them, hollowing out, we are going to leave until later, the reason being that the spindle

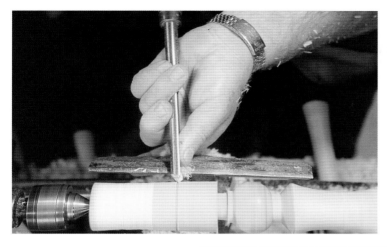

Fig. 23 (Left) Entry for a gouge cut at the start of a cove is the same as for a skew facing cut. The index finger under the rest pinches the blade which is vertical and is at a perfect right angle to the face of the spindle.

(Below) The cove is developing. From the entry facing cut the blade is rolled and the handle begins to drop as the edge starts to move upwards.

*Fig. 24 (Below left) Starting the other side of the cove with another entry cut.
(Below right) The cove is completed with the gouge rolled onto its back and the bevel running out over the base of the cove.*

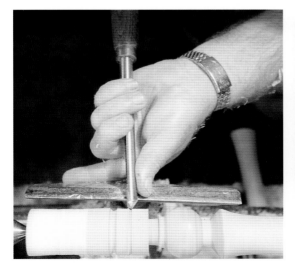

turner's interest in hollowing-out is substantially very different from that of the bowl turner's in that it not only involves turning and cutting methods, but also scraping and drilling out.

GROOVING AND SIZING CUTS

This leaves us with grooving, and here there are two aspects to look at. One we have already touched on under facing cuts, and this is the vee groove. The vee groove is made with the skew (or the beading and parting tool) in the facing-cut position and is done by first making an entry cut in line with the bottom of the required vee. The skew goes straight in at right-angles to the axis and you then take facing cuts first on one side and then on the other of the entry cut until you have widened the groove to the required size and vee profile. If you tried to make the first entry at an angle down one side of the vee, the skew would kick sideways.

SIZING A REQUIRED DIAMETER

The second aspect of grooving is much more important: it is done with a parting tool and is most often undertaken to size down a cylinder to a required diameter; and for this task we also need a set of external callipers.

Sizing the diameter of a length of cylinder is usually done by cutting a number of grooves of measured depth, which are then joined by planing away the wood between. This is the method that is used when you want to produce a spindle of uniform diameter. The same approach is used to define the maximum diameter of a feature. So before we start cutting, say, a bead, we might first put a sizing groove at the centre – or maximum diameter – point of the bead, and also two depth grooves to delineate the width of the bead.

DEFINING THE BOUNDARIES OF A FEATURE

The other use of sizing grooves is therefore to define the boundaries of a feature, and so after the maximum diameter groove at the apex of the bead, we would then cut two deeper grooves, one at each end of the length of the bead. These would mark the minimum diameter, and we would round into them when cutting the bead's profile. Equally, when cutting a fillet to separate two features we would usually cut the fillet first as a sizing groove, and would then work the feature ends down to the fillet.

THE PARTING TOOL

Sizing grooves are made with the parting tool, a narrow but deep-bladed chisel, the cutting edge of which is only ⅛ to ³⁄₁₆in (4 to 5mm) long – although the blade in cross-section may be ¾in (20mm) wide. The edge is square to the blade, but this time across the blade section, and the tool is always held on its side so that the edge cuts straight across the top of the grain – the very plane in which we said a skew chisel would roll fibres off the surface. Here, however, there is little tearing – provided the tool is kept sharp – because you are cutting a deep but narrow groove, and whole fibres cannot now be rolled off because their ends are held firmly in place.

Most parting tools have profiled sections. Some have a wedge end so that the cutting tip is wider than the blade, others are diamond-section; both of these have the advantage of reduced side-wall friction. Another type of parter has a wedge section with a hollow ground lower edge; this gives two points which cut through the fibres more cleanly.

The side of the blade is supported on the tool-rest, and the rest is positioned a little above axis height. The long bevel rests on the top of the cylinder, and the tool is then

Fig. 25 Entry for a diamond point parting tool. The bevel is rubbing and the blade is then drawn back.

drawn back until cutting begins. As the blade moves into the wood, so the heel of the tool handle is lifted. If you continue the cut right through the cylinder, you have, in effect, parted off: you have cut the cylinder in two, and this is the way that we finish off the spindle to remove it from the lathe.

CUTTING TO A REQUIRED DIAMETER

However, we do not yet want to go that far, but wish to cut the groove to a required diameter. To do this, take a pair of external callipers and open the jaws to the diameter required. This can be done by checking

Fig. 26 Sizing cut with a parting tool and external callipers.

the gape against a ruler; by opening the jaws against a full-sized drawing; or opening them against a pattern piece, spigot, drill bit, gauge or whatever.

The parting tool is held in the right hand, and the left hand holds the callipers lightly against the far side of the rotating cylinder; as the groove develops, the jaws run in this. When the required diameter has been reached, the jaws will slip across the centre of the cylinder; cutting pressure is immediately lifted off the parting tool, as the required diameter has now been achieved.

It should be noted that some external callipers have chisel-like points to the jaws, and these can catch as the wood is roughened by the parting tool. It is therefore advisable to file the jaws of your sizing callipers to a nice smooth round.

A WORD OF CAUTION

It is worth sounding a note of caution. Most external callipers have a screw adjustment controlling the gape. When the jaws are running in the groove before the required diameter is reached, they are running on a fast-rotating wooden surface and there is some vibration in the tool. This can be enough to cause the jaws to slowly open. If what you are trying to size is an absolutely critical dimension – as with, say, a spigot to fit tight into a socket – then the moment the callipers pass across, indicating that the required diameter has been reached, remove them and check the setting. You may find the gap has opened slightly, in which case you will need to readjust the callipers and take a final, careful cut.

Calliper sizing can be extremely accurate, provided it is done carefully and is checked. Many turners set the callipers wide on the basis that they can then clean up and achieve the required diameter. However, more often than not the 'clearing up' takes the diameter to less than that required, and a sloppy fit is achieved. Do the job properly, have confidence in what you are doing, and you won't need to clean up because you will be right nine times out of ten; whereas the cleaning-up approach will probably give you only a three out of ten success rate! As ever, the old adage applies: *measure* twice and cut *once*!

Fig. 27 Using a beading and parting tool to make wider grooves.

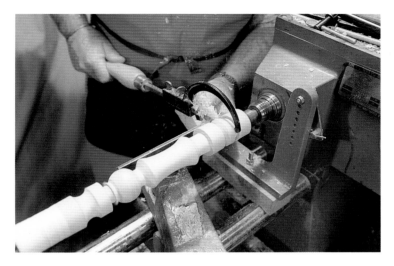

Fig. 28 Making a sizing groove with a beading and parting tool using a bedan to control the diameter.

SIZING WITH A BEDAN

This is one area in which a useful gadget has been developed: a device that replaces the callipers, to be used with a ⅜in (9mm) square beading and parting tool. The 'calliper' part is called a bedan and it clamps onto a standard beading and parting tool blade: by moving the clamping position it can be reset to any required groove diameter. Now as the groove is cut, you remove wood until the snout of the calliper drops over the diameter.

MARKING SIZING POINTS

The sizing points are first marked on the spindle. This can be done with the lathe stopped by first using a ruler to fix the key points, and then marking clearly by holding a soft lead pencil (a carpenter's pencil is ideal) against the wood while the lathe is running.

It is strongly recommended that you develop a standard procedure for the marking of sizing points. Where exactness is not required you may merely put a pencil mark in the approximate required position and then rest the parting tool somewhere on this mark. If you need an exact position for a groove – as in making copies or fixing a required length – you must mark the exact position and then cut precisely to the mark. You may decide to mark the inboard edge of the groove, the outboard, or *both* edges: the important thing is to adopt your own preference and then *always* work to that. Personally I like the inboard edge for a groove of parting-tool blade width; and then both edges for wider grooves.

When cutting very wide grooves the beading and parting tool is often used, and two adjacent grooves are developed together to prevent any tool binding.

With all forms of parting and beading tool we still adopt the basic rule of bevel rubbing. The cut is started with the bevel resting on the cylinder, and the tool handle is then drawn back until the cut begins. The bevel rub is then maintained as the tool bites deeper into the groove.

FINISHING OFF

Let's take the use of this tool to its conclusion. It is called a parting tool because it is often used to part right through the timber

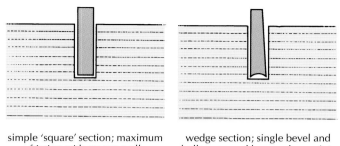

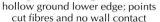

simple 'square' section; maximum friction with groove wall

wedge section; single bevel and hollow ground lower edge; points cut fibres and no wall contact

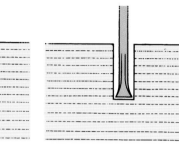

diamond section; double bevel; minimal wall contact

fan tail tip; double bevel; no wall contact

Fig. 29 Parting tool sections.

(Below) *Fig. 30 Completion of parting off: the left hand catches the spindle as it breaks free. A better finish is achieved if the last nub is cut through with a skew facing cut.*

– that is, to cut the spindle off to a required length when all other turning is completed. This is done with the lathe still turning. The groove is continued into the wood until very little is left. At this point the fingers of the left hand are loosely wrapped round the spindle. As the last nub of wood is turned away the unrestrained spindle would fly off; however, the left hand is there to prevent this, to catch it, and to remove it from the turning lathe.

And that is it – all the basic cuts ever used during the turning of the external profiles of cylinders. With these you can complete every shape on the composite cylinder we started off with –

that is, all but one: the missing element is hollowing out, and a cut of this nature is required for the beak; but more of that later.

— 4 —

MAKING SHAPES

The cutting principles that we have now established are the fundamentals of all turning. As we have seen, almost every tool used in spindle turning can be considered as a skew chisel that has been modified or shaped in some way to suit a particular application. 'Scrapers', so much loved in the school woodwork room, have virtually no place in spindle turning. So if we understand the principles of skew use we can effectively use any turning tool and complete most turning tasks. The next stage is to consider how the cuts are put into practice in producing specific decorative profiles, and to look at some of the problems we encounter.

TURNING LONG, THIN SPINDLES

First there are some basic issues concerning grain orientation and the mechanics of turning long, thin items.

THE IMPORTANCE OF TRUE-RUNNING GRAIN

In the first chapter, when looking at the fundamental process of cutting wood with a skew chisel, we saw how important it was that the run of the grain was true to the axis of the spindle, and that it didn't have any wild variations; so let us explore this a little further. There are two major issues: first, many spindles have a structural function, and you don't want them to be forever breaking in the middle. They are often fairly thin at various points, and if the grain is not true, breakage is inevitable, taking the form of a long diagonal split along the lie of the grain.

A further problem is that the moment you start to apply decoration you are cutting across and even into the fibres. Thus on a piece of timber with wild grain, you could be cutting downhill on one part of the revolution and uphill on the next; thus it would be almost impossible to get good crisp detail on whatever feature you were trying to cut if you had an area of uphill grain on what was a downhill profile. So we must have clean timber which is knot-free and which has straight grain running true along the axis of the spindle.

But this is only the start of our mechanical difficulties, because the most significant problem area to be addressed when turning spindles, particularly thin or 'fine' ones, concerns flexing and vibration.

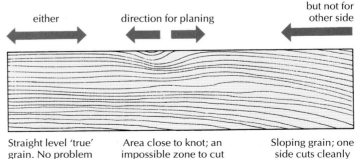

either   direction for planing   but not for other side

Straight level 'true' grain. No problem planing in either direction.

Area close to knot; an impossible zone to cut cleanly.

Sloping grain; one side cuts cleanly other side tears.

Fig. 31 Planing with the grain.

OVERCOMING VIBRATION AND FLEXING

You have a long, relatively thin piece of wood which is compressed at both ends as it is pinched between the drive spur and the tailstock point. You then spin this at high speed. In such a set-up, there are many of the basic characteristics of the strings of a musical instrument, namely that it does not take much to cause the wood to flex and to vibrate. Vibration and flexing are problems that we shall be looking at in greater depth later, but for the moment we need to consider the fact that the smaller we make the diameter at any point along the length of the spindle, the greater will be the flexing and vibration. Moreover, the nearer the thin sections are to the centre of the length of the spindle, the worse it will be, and if you try to work on the spindle on the outboard side of any thin section you will find the vibration tendency increases.

For this reason spindles (and the stems of goblets and suchlike) are always worked from the outboard (the tailstock) end first: you finish off the outermost feature before you move to the next feature towards the drive end. You will be tempted for many reasons to work the whole length of the spindle as a piece, possibly to cut all the fillets first, then maybe to round all the beads before going back to work on all the coves. However, this would introduce thin diameter sections along the spindle's length, and if you then tried to work any one feature outboard of a thinned section you would increase the vibration tendency.

So we have a rule, which is to complete each outboard end feature before moving on to the adjacent inboard one; work the spindle from right to left. It is a 'flexible rule', however, and later, as you learn to be able to assess diameters and timbers, you may decide to take reasonable short cuts. As far as I am concerned, when the minimum diameter of any feature (including grooves and fillets) is less than a tenth of the total length of the spindle, then the rule applies. So a 10in (25cm) spindle of 1in (25mm) diameter would be just acceptable, but a couple more inches in length and I would work to the rule. Alternatively I might call into use a 'long work steady', a piece of equipment we will be considering in more detail later on.

CUTTING MULTI-FEATURED SPINDLES

The importance of what is being said here is paramount because it must condition the whole working procedure. Except on one occasion throughout the section on roughing, sizing and planing, we have implied that the whole blank is turned to a cylinder and that this work should be completed before any features are cut. Often this will be the case, *but* there are times when this is not so. For instance, many furniture legs have a square section at one end and some have squares at both ends, so that the frame members can abut into a nice tight joint. Often the head of the leg will later have mortise slots cut into it. The blank has to be of the required size of square section and this is left untouched in the turning process. In such cases only the centre length is roughed to a round.

So we usually start a spindle by planing the cylinder section to a diameter that corresponds with the maximum diameter we will require, namely the diameter of the largest bead or other feature. To do this we first turn a small area (a groove) down to the required diameter at a few marker points. On a relatively short spindle this is likely to be the two ends of the cylindrical section, and then somewhere near the mid-point; with longer spindles it may be the ends and three or four places down its length. Use the parting tool and a set of external callipers, as described earlier.

Fig. 32 Except on very robust, short spindles, detail is always cut by working in from the tailstock end.

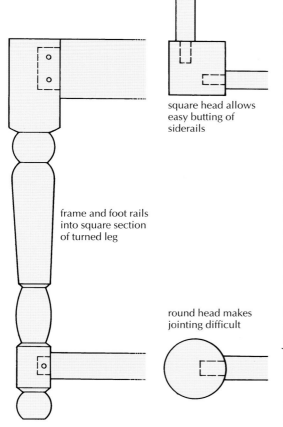

square head allows easy butting of siderails

frame and foot rails into square section of turned leg

round head makes jointing difficult

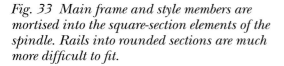

Fig. 33 Main frame and style members are mortised into the square-section elements of the spindle. Rails into rounded sections are much more difficult to fit.

So we have a complete cylinder or a piece that has a cylindrical centre section with a square element at one or both ends. The piece now has to be marked up for the next stage of the process.

MARKING KEY FEATURES

When cutting a multi-featured spindle, particularly when it is to be one of a matched set, it is important that having rounded to a cylinder, you mark accurately the exact locations of the beginning and end of any key diameters and the locations of each of the features. From here on, we can focus upon the application of our seven basic cuts in the cutting of the features used in decoration: it is back to the composite spindle that was defined earlier.

As was said then, no one would make such a spindle; so if you wish to practise any of the cuts, mount shorter pieces of timber and just try cutting only two or three of the features on any one piece of timber. And immediately we are going to bend our rules!

When you have a square to round, the square will almost always have a cross-section width which is greater than the diameter of any part of the cylinder. So assuming a square at both ends of the spindle, it would be in order to finish off both round-to-square joints – including the inboard end – before working on any other feature.

45

THE SQUARE-TO-ROUND INTERFACE

There are two possible approaches to starting the square-to-round interface, one which could be described as 'easy', the other 'problematical'. First, mark on the square blank before any roughing, the approximate position of the bottom of the shoulder; on our spindle this is where the shoulder meets the large bead. Next wrap from two to four turns of masking tape over the mark, allowing at least 1in (25mm) of tape on the square section and ½in (12mm) or so to the bead side. Now carefully re-mark the location of the groove on the top of the masking tape: measure it and locate it precisely and continue it right round the blank. The purpose of this masking tape is to prevent the corners of the squared section breaking out when you start working.

In the 'easy' method you now make a saw cut on the mark on each corner to a depth of about two thirds of the shoulder. You can then rough and plane the cylinder part, and finally round over the corners of the square section using a facing cut.

The 'problematical' method is the one normally used by skilled turners. Here no saw cut is made, nor is the cylinder roughed. The step by step procedure is as follows:

1. Put the tool-rest at centre height and position it to just miss the rotating corners. Set the lathe speed to 700–800rpm.
2. Wrap three or four turns of masking tape around at the interface.
3. Draw the exact location of the deepest point A, and limit of the shoulder at B onto the masking tape (all the way round the spindle).
4. Start the lathe. Hold the skew on its edge on the rest, with the long point down, and using the pinch grip. Position skew at right-angles to the axis of the wood at A, and hold it parallel to the ground.
5. Advance the point slowly but firmly into the wood until resistance prevents it entering further. Withdraw the point.
6. Angle the skew slightly to the axis, and from the right side of the groove towards the outboard end; take off the tip of the corner with a facing cut.
7. Move the skew 1mm to the right, and maintaining the angle to the axis, take another facing cut off the corner.
8. Repeat this several times to widen the gap.
9. Move to the left of the groove at B and repeat steps 6, 7 and 8, but to the left of the groove (towards the inboard end).
10. For the final cuts, enter at the angle of the shoulder at B and using a facing cut with the skew leaning over 1–2 degrees, make a single smooth cut right down into the bottom of the groove.

This is not an easy process, although much of the difficulty is psychological! On the entry and the first few cuts you are advancing the skew point into the shadowy penumbra created by the rotating corners, so you cannot really see where you are going. Also,

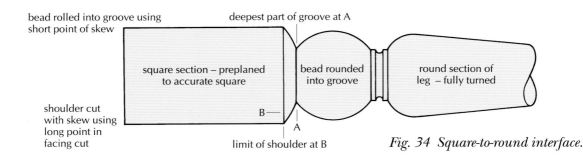

bead rolled into groove using short point of skew

deepest part of groove at A

square section – preplaned to accurate square

bead rounded into groove

round section of leg – fully turned

shoulder cut with skew using long point in facing cut

B

A

limit of shoulder at B

Fig. 34 Square-to-round interface.

each time the wood hits the blade there is a heavy knock, and this can be quite alarming. Moreover, you only have to have the skew mis-angled a fraction and you can tear a splinter off a corner you are trying to protect. For this reason, after making the entry cut and the first vee groove with the skew, many turners prefer to change to a shallow U-gouge used in a facing-cut position.

Before finishing rounding off the shoulders on the square section, you may prefer to rough and plane the cylinder.

PLANING THE CYLINDER

1. Set the tool-rest to just above the height of the centre axis of the wood. Keep the lathe speed to 700–800rpm.
2. Start the lathe and take up the roughing gouge. At the left end of the tool-rest, rest the back of the blade on the tool-rest and the blade near the tip on the rotating wood, angling the tool slightly to the left and with the U of the gouge leaning to the left by 10 to 15 degrees.
3. Draw the blade back until the bevel comes into contact, then slightly further until cutting begins.
4. Sweep the tool to the left towards the left end of the tool-rest in a continuous cut.
5. Angle the tool to the right and make a rightwards pass.
6. Continue sweeping in one direction and then the other until a thumb test shows that the cylinder is smooth.
7. By repositioning the rest, bring the whole spindle from the square-section groove to the outboard end to a smooth cylinder.
8. Stop the lathe and increase the speed to between 1,250 and 1,500rpm.
9. Now with a parting tool and callipers, size the cylinder to the diameter you are going to work to. On the test spindle this will be the maximum diameter of the big bead (and the shoulder of the taper).

10. Reposition the tool-rest to just below the level of the top of the cylinder, and close it in until the gap is about $\frac{3}{16}$in (5mm).
11. Start the lathe. With the skew chisel at the left-hand end of the rest, place it so that the blade also rests across the top of the spindle, with the long point towards the far side of the lathe. Angle the tool so that the cutting edge is at 45 degrees to the axis of the spindle. Now draw the blade back until the bevel rubs and the cut begins.
12. With a light grip, sweep the skew to the right in a continuous cut to the right-hand end of the rest. Take care that the tool does not fall off the end.
13. Change hands, and sweep the skew back from right to left.
14. Reposition the tool-rest down the length until the cylinder is smooth and even from groove A to the outboard end.

If you have not already done so, finish off the shoulders of the square section. This can now be done without moving the rest from the planing position by using the U-gouge and rolling over.

While we are talking about square-to-round there is another point to watch: it is to be hoped that you can clamp up your tool-rest so that if you lean against the end of it accidentally, it will not budge. There is nothing worse than getting a nice square-to-round interface only to then lean against the tool-rest and cause one end of it to move into the flight path of a square corner. Once you have cut the interface, always try to position the tool-rest so that even if it does move accidentally, it will not catch a corner of the square section.

Now, following the rule, we move to the outboard end. Here (for some inexplicable reason) we have a feature used on a tool handle: a spigot clad with a ferrule.

SIZING THE SPIGOT AND FIXING A FERRULE ON THE WASTE END

1. Cut a short length of 1¼in (28mm) copper waterpipe and deburr the cut ends. Set a pair of external callipers to the inside diameter of the pipe. Open the callipers a quarter turn on the thumb screw; this will make the wood spigot slightly oversize.

2. Set the tool-rest just above axis height and 5mm from the cylinder, and the lathe speed at 1,000–1,500rpm. Start the lathe.

3. Using the callipers and a parting tool, you are going to size the spigot to the immediate right of the outermost feature (the last bead on the spindle).

4. Position the parting tool on its side on the rest with the bevel rubbing on the surface of the cylinder, and the blade at a right-angle to the spindle's axis.

5. Draw the tool back until cutting commences.

6. Continue drawing the tool back slowly and raising the butt of the handle as it cuts a groove in the cylinder.

7. With the left hand, hold the callipers in the groove ahead of the cutting edge as you continue to cut in with the parting tool held in the right.

8. The instant that the callipers slide over the spindle lift off the parting tool.

9. Take up the beading and parting tool, and again using the callipers, size down the end of the spigot just inboard of the tailstock point. The position of the tool-rest and the lathe speed remain as for the parting-tool groove.

10. Put down the callipers, and using the beading and parting tool, remove the timber between the two sizing grooves. Now angle the B & P tool to 45 degrees to the axis with the cutting edge leading to the right; use the tool as a skew to slightly taper down the spigot to the outboard end.

11. Stop the lathe and wind out the tailstock point, and offer up the ferrule: it will probably go a centimetre or two onto the spigot. Leave it in place and clamp up the tailstock. Restart the lathe, and using the B & P tool at right-angles to the axis dress, the spigot with a planing cut until the ferrule can be tapped up against the face.

The next feature inboard is a sequence of beads and a reed.

CUTTING BEADS AND A REED

1. With the parting tool and callipers, locate and size the outboard end of the scotia.

2. Divide the cylinder where the beads are to be cut into a number of equal-width rings; including the reed, four are shown in Fig. 36. Pencil-mark the grooves between each element.

3. Position the tool-rest for a facing cut, and with the long point of the skew, make grooves to define the location of the grooves between the beads.

4. Raise the tool-rest to a centimetre below the top of the cylinder, and ³⁄₁₆in (5mm) out from the surface. (The gap may have to be wider – it will depend upon your tool-rest profile.)

5. With the beading and parting tool at an angle of about 45 degrees to the spindle's axis and resting on a corner, cut the shoulders off the skew-cut grooves. You will be cutting into the wood with the corner of the B & P so you will need a firm grip to overcome the tendency to kick back.

6. Widen these cuts working from one side and then the other, until each groove is vee-shaped.

7. Now position the B & P as if it were a skew, with the bevel rubbing on the top of the cylinder at the apex of the bead, and roll the cut down into the groove. You will probably need to make a number of

Fig. 35 Cutting a bead with a beading and parting tool. With this tool the corner can be dug in to start the rounding process.

passes to get the grooves between the beads deep enough, and to get a nice regular curve on the face of each bead.

8. Lower the tool-rest to the facing-cut position, and with a skew with the long point down, cut the shoulders of the disc that is to be the reed.

9. Continue making angled facing cuts to complete both faces of the reed.

NOTE: You could also cut this reed using the beading and parting tool to make what are, in effect, flat-sided beads.

Mention must also be made here of the bead-cutting tools that are now available from a number of makers. These are single-bevel blades, the underside of which are ground to a semicircular groove (obviously the size of bead is governed entirely by the size of the tool employed). Ashley Isles, one of the best of tool suppliers, offers bead cutters in two sizes: 6mm and 7mm wide. Sorby, also known for their quality tools, sell a kit with a bead cutter and two captive ring tools.

The tool is offered across the top of the zone to be cut with the bevel of the edge uppermost. This time it is the wings of the concave section which rest on the timber to provide the initial 'bevel-rubbing' contact. The blade is then brought back until cutting commences and the edge arcs down into the wood.

Obviously the huge disadvantage of bead-cutting tools is that the size of bead you cut is fixed by the size of the tool. The great advantage is that they produce nice symmetrical beads of a small size; it is just these sizes of beads that are the most difficult to cut cleanly with skews or B & P tools.

CUTTING THE SCOTIA

1. Mark off the inboard end fillet and size it down to its finished diameter with the parting tool and callipers.

Fig. 36 A small-diameter, fingernail gouge cutting into a corner.

2. Mark where the fillet starts to sweep down the cove.

NOTE: The shallow entry angle of the cove means that it is not cut with a vertical entry cut, but is developed back from the outboard end.

3. Position the tool-rest about one third below the height of the top of the finished feature.
4. With a shallow, U, fingernail profile gouge, start to taper down the reed end of the scotia.
5. Continue working back towards the fillet with a slight scooping motion.

CUTTING THE OVOLO

Here we are going to work two features together, as they start with similar diameters.

1. Mark the outboard end of the beak, and size down the cylindrical section from here outboard to the scotia fillet using a parting tool, callipers and a skew.
2. With the tool-rest positioned for a facing cut and the skew long point down, make a facing cut where the ovolo meets the short cylinder. This is the first quirk.
3. At the outboard end of the ovolo cut another quirk onto the face of the fillet; the vee here develops inboard.
4. Raise the tool-rest to about one third below the top.
5. Round the two shoulders with a skew. The inboard end has a sharper radius than the outboard.
6. The outboard end has a smaller radius, and the face of the quirk now needs to be cleaned up with a true facing cut.

A True Facing Cut

1. With the tool-rest at or just below the axis, make a facing cut to clean up the wall inboard of the fillet.

2. Position the skew on its edge, long point down and angled so that the bevel is in the same plane as the groove face. Now take the handle a fraction further out towards the outboard end, angling the bevel a mere half degree to the face to be cut. At the same time lean the blade over by 1 to 2 degrees from the vertical so the upper short point is just clear of the face.
3. Advance the tool in towards the centre. Keep it parallel to the ground, and keep the bevel rubbing. You should take off a tiny circular shaving and leave a burnished face.
4. This cut should have removed the corner shaving left from the previous ovolo cut. If it has not, clean into the corner with the point of the skew. The aim is for a perfect, crisp right-angled corner.

GROOVED CYLINDER AND COVE

1. Move to the short cylindrical section, and using a parting tool (and callipers), cut the simple, square-sided groove.
2. We now have to size down the inboard end of the cove, and then to cut a cove which is similar to the scotia except that the curve is sharper and the entry is made with a facing cut. Mark where the concave starts.
3. Working from the outboard end of the cove, set the tool-rest just below axis height and position a fingernail profiled gouge on its side opposite the line, with the U facing inboard. This is the entry position for cutting a half cove. The tool starts parallel to the ground and at right-angles to the spindle's axis.
4. Remember there is a tendency to kick sideways if the cutting edge is not vertical, so hold the tool in a pinch grip.
5. Advance the edge into the spindle, and immediately cutting commences, start the scooping motion of cove cutting. This means push the handle forwards, at the same time lowering the butt and

rotating the blade so that it finishes lying on its back on the tool-rest with the blade pointing upwards and the bevel on the top of the lowest point of the cove.

6. The final cut – in which the side of the fingernail ends up against the face of the beak – may leave a small flake of swarf in the corner.

CUTTING THE BEAK

There are two ways of cutting the beak: the one on this spindle is shallow and may be completed using a U-gouge to make slightly scooped facing cuts. Rest and tool positions are similar to skew-made facing cuts. We will later consider the use of a bowl gouge.

AN OGEE: A COMBINED CONCAVE AND CONVEX FORM

1. First define the inner limit of the next feature, then cut a fillet at the inboard end with parting tool and callipers. This will later be scooped out to a cove.
2. The ogee feature starts with a flattened bead and then sweeps into a shallow cove. However, the cove's radius may be too sharp to skew-cut, so the feature is cut with a fingernail gouge used as a skew chisel.
3. Remember to cut downhill on both sides of the cove.
4. The tool-rest should be positioned one third below the top, and that part of the cutting edge of the gouge which is in contact with the wood should be kept at 45 degrees to the axis.

THE LOZENGE WITH INCISED FEATURES

1. We have already done all of the cuts involved in this figure, but here a couple of additional problems have been introduced. First, fix the inboard end using a

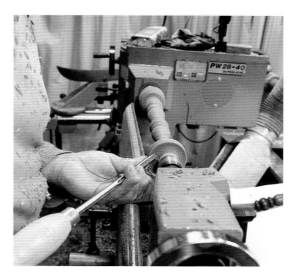

Fig. 37 Hollowing a beak with a small bowl gouge.

parting tool to groove what will be a short cylinder (an extended fillet).

2. Form the lozenge with a skew, working first towards the outboard end and then rounding the inboard end. Problem one is to ensure that it is truly symmetrical, with both ends having precisely the same curve. If you cannot achieve this by eye, use drawing instruments to produce a cardboard (or plywood) template. Templates are often used for turning bowling balls and the like, where curve symmetry is of paramount importance.
3. In making the template, check that it is accurate by testing it both ways round against an instrument-drawn line.
4. The centre vee groove is cut using a skew in the facing-cut mode. No problems here.
5. Now to the two coves. Both are cut into a curving face. Previously the coves were cut into a parallel section of the cylinder, and the entry, at right angles to the surface, was easy to achieve as it was also at right-angles to the whole axis. To make the entry on these angled coves, the

fingernail gouge cut is again started with the tool on its side and the edge vertical, but you now have to position the tool so that the blade is at right-angles to the surface of the lozenge at the exact point of entry. The scooping and the cutting from both sides down to the bottom of the cove is then standard. It does, however, require extra care to get a nicely profiled, truly semicircular cove.

6. Finally, cut a simple cove into the outboard end fillet, but leave two tiny fillets at each end of the cove. You will need a very small gouge to cut this cove and trim the fillets out with a parting tool.

A FULL BEAD

1. We are now somewhere near the midpoint along the length of the spindle. This is the area where flexing and vibration can become a problem, and here we are going to cut a true, full bead of less than the maximum diameter of the spindle. With a bead of this size you have a choice between using a beading and parting tool or a small-width (about ⅝in/15mm) skew; it is easier with the skew.

   In essence, provided you have access space, the bigger the skew (within reason) the easier it is to roll beads.

2. With the tool-rest just above axis height, cut a sizing groove to the inboard end of the bead's length. This will be to the finished size of the fillet. In defining the lozenge, we cut the inboard end cylinder which now forms the outboard end of the bead.

3. With the parting tool and callipers, reduce the diameter of the bead cylinder to the required bead diameter.

4. Mark the centre of the bead with a pencil ring.

5. Raise the rest to about half the bead's height. Starting with the skew half-way between the centre line and the groove,

make a rolling-over cut removing the corner of the groove.

6. Make the next cut a little closer to the centre mark.

7. The final cut should start on the mark and roll right down to the finished diameter of the groove.

8. Work the other side in a similar manner, rounding down to the outboard cylinder section.

At first you may find it a little difficult to get symmetry between both walls of the bead, but again, practice will make perfect.

CUTTING A BOBBIN

1. Bring the tool-rest back down to about half-way between the top of the cylinder and the spindle's axis. Now reduce the short cylinder length of the inboard end of the bobbin to its finished diameter and length. To do this, put a sizing groove at each end with the parting tool and callipers, then remove the timber between with a beading and parting tool.

2. Now reduce the bobbin section to its required maximum diameter (the apex of the two end wings). The roughing gouge could take the surplus off quickly, but as you already have the beading and parting tool in your hand, use that as a skew.

3. With the B & P take off the end corners to produce the sloping section. The tool will be held with a corner of the blade resting on the tool-rest so that the cutting edge is at the angle required for the slope of the shoulders. The corner of the edge is pushed into the wood to take the corner off in a single pass.

4. To cut the concave section, try using a square-ended gouge and start with planing cuts from the apex of the wings (with the bevel rubbing and a 45-degree angle). Cut downhill from one end and then the other, with the cuts meeting in the centre of the concave.

5. Make sure that the slopes on both sides of the centre are symmetrical.

NOTE: A fairly shallow concave of this nature may be cut with a small skew once your skew-planing skills are developed. You may also, of course, use a fingernail profile, shallow U-gouge.

A FREE-STANDING SEMICIRCULAR BEAD

1. Define the inboard end with a parting tool and calliper groove – although by this stage along the spindle you could probably get the diameter right by eye, without the callipers.
2. Reduce the short section of cylinder now produced to the required maximum diameter using a B & P tool. Then for the next step, set the tool-rest to about a centimetre below the top of the reduced cylinder.
3. The bead is now 'rolled'. First cut away corner is with the point of the tool – hold the tool firmly with the cutting edge angled diagonally upwards. Now start with the tool flat on the rest with a definite bevel rub; as the cut commences, start to roll the tool on its axis so that the cutting edge moves from horizontal to near-vertical. Make sure that the cut is kept in the centre of the cutting edge, which is positioned at 45 degrees to the axis of the spindle; a moment's inattention will cause you to peel off a layer from the top of the bead and so leave a flat.
4. As you roll the tool into the corner where the bead meets the main cylinder you still keep the bevel rubbing, but you move the cut from the centre of the edge towards the leading point, at the same time increasing the edge-to-axis angle – this produces a clean right-angle as you have moved into what is almost a facing cut. This will mean the butt of the tool handle is now high over the top of the spindle.

THE TAPERED SECTION WITH TOP END OVOLO

1. With the tool-rest about a centimetre below the top of the cylinder, the whole of this feature is produced using a medium-to-broad skew chisel.
2. Mark off with a pencil ring the apex of the convex section behind the ovolo (the shoulder), and the boundaries of the fillet groove between the shoulder and the final bead. Size this groove with parting tool and callipers.
3. Make the first skew planing cut close to the outboard end bead, and move the start of each subsequent planing cut up towards the apex of the taper. Don't forget the rules: the long point is on top, the bevel is rubbing, there is a 45-degree edge-to-axis angle, the tool blade is flat on the rest and the top of the timber, you have a gentle grasp of the skew handle, and the steadying fingers of your left hand rest lightly on the top of the blade. Work in nice, long, continuous sweeps.
4. Rounding over the shoulder with the skew differs from the rounding over of the previous bead with the B & P tool. Thus you do not take the corner off with the point but instead start with the blade flat, and gradually roll it onto its leading side. The corner is therefore slowly worked away, rather than being peeled off.
5. Also, as the handle is lifted and the edge works towards the vertical cut deep inside, you maintain the cut in the centre of the edge. If the lower point *does* catch there will be a dig-in, and a spiral groove which will spin up right across the apex of the shoulder. Here again, the arc-profiled skews are much less prone to catching.
6. Having set the tool-rest just below the top of the spindle (⅜in/10mm down), it is probable that the groove at the inboard end of the feature will finish below the rest height.

7. The last few cuts into this groove will be cutting down to the fillet ring left by the sizing groove. This may push up some swarf in the hollow. To remove this, invert the skew so that the long point is now at the bottom. Make a slightly angled facing cut into the outboard end wall of the groove to cut the swarf free.

THE FINAL BEAD

1. This is just a slightly bigger version of the mid-point bead, and is cut in exactly the same way with a medium skew.
2. As you near completion you will probably have to remove swarf from the inboard end groove, and take a light facing cut to dress the face of the bead and that of the round-to-square shoulder. Both may be done with the skew, long point down, and the tool-rest back down to axis height. However as we said when we first cut the square-to-round, beginners may find it easier to dress this face with a fingernail-profile, shallow U-gouge.

CONCLUSION

In working through the steps of cutting the features on a spindle, we have dealt with each in textbook style. The ideal tool and tool-rest position has been stated, and warnings have been given on critical points. We have seen that on occasions there are alternative approaches, particularly in relation to the tool chosen: some are easier, and some are for the expert. It is up to you to choose which route you take, but it is strongly recommended that, in time, you develop skills across all the options.

On occasions in these notes we have mentioned the size of the spindle being turned, and most of the illustrations have been based on a spindle of about 2in (50mm) in diameter. We did also say that on really tiny beads you might round using a parting tool.

At each stage we have been looking at the basic principles which apply whatever the diameter of the spindle. The only thing that might change is the size of tool used – and only tool sizes (and the size of lathe) differ between the working of a four-poster bed-leg, a refectory table pedestal or a lace bobbin! Obviously the bobbin will require greater delicacy of touch and a much higher speed of rotation to get a good finish.

Any spindle turner has the ability to make a lace bobbin, and there are no different cuts to those we have now detailed. Some find that such fine, gentle work is a pleasant foil to the hours spent making bigger pieces. Some turners go even smaller, making tableware items for dolls' houses; and even smaller. When you get to this size of work you often have to devise your own tools – thus masonry nails can be ground to effective micro scrapers. Mind you, the great American turner Dell Stubbs has a good party piece: he sometimes turns a micro goblet using a side-axe as a cutter!

Clearly, making a spindle – bed leg or bobbin, full size or miniature – in the ways described, with constant tool changes and frequent movements of the tool-rest position, can take a considerable time. In reality, experienced spindle turners take many short cuts and compromises. Some may just make one or two tool-rest position changes, and a talented few only ever use one, or at most two tools. Some do not stop the lathe for a whole shift – not even to put a new blank on for the next spindle – and they rough to a round, plane, roll over and cut out coves all with one size of skew and a gouge! For the less experienced it is recommended that you do use the 'correct' tools; but as you do so, think through what is happening, and try to understand why the tools are different and what advantages the differences give you. In the end it is that understanding which enables you to develop the skills to do fine and complex work, whether you choose to use one or twenty tools.

(Top) *Fig. 38 Various chisels. From the right: standard square-bladed skew; oval skew with straight edge; two arc-ground skews; parting tool with wide point; beading and parting tool; diamond-section parter; bowl gouge.*

(Middle) *Fig. 39 Shallow U-gouges. From the right: modern fingernail gouge; two old carbon steel gouges (wonderful!); four spindle gouges with point to fingernail ends.*

(Bottom) *Fig. 40 Deep U-gouges. Various sizes and end grinds for bowl gouges. Some are also used for roughing small-diameter spindles.*

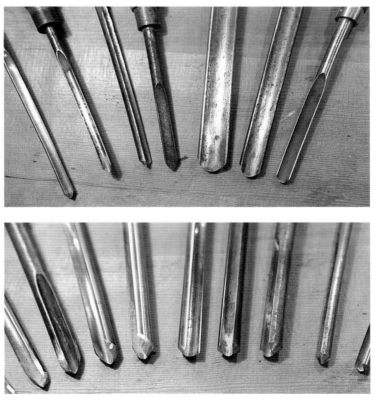

One thing is certain: in recent years suppliers have brought out many new tools and gismos – some are variations on existing ones; some unique, new specials. Most are useful as they enable us to accomplish some quite difficult tasks with relative ease. However none are really necessary, and in the worst instances they use inappropriate methods to achieve a result that would make a skilled turner shudder. A typical example is a scraper-based tool to produce crude, rough captive rings – but more of this later!

To conclude, the tools used in producing the various shapes are summarized in the table overleaf. Included in this are recommendations on the types and sizes of tools that make up a comprehensive kit. Figures are given for the suggested bevel grinding angles (we will consider these angles again when we look at tool sharpening).

Table 1

Class	*Tool Name*	*Blade Section*	*Sizes Used*	*Basic Kit*	*Edge Profile*	*Edge Axis*	*Bevel*	*Basic Grind*	*Use*
scraper	captive ring tool	oval	¼ to ½in		Semicircular		Compound		Making captive rings on spindles
scraper	square-ended scraper	rectangular	⅛ to 2in	⅛. ½in	Square to axis	90 deg	40 to 75 deg	70 deg	Cleaning square corners. Dressing beads (if you have to!)
scraper	round-nosed scraper	rectangular	⅛ to 2in	⅛. ¾in	Gently rounded	70 to 70 deg	40 to 75 deg	70 deg	Detailing. Dressing coves
scraper	diamond point scraper	rectangular	½in	½in	Pointed	45/45 deg	60 to 75 deg	70 deg	Small vee grooves. Dressing and undercutting corners
gouge	roughing gouge	deep double U	¾ to 2in	1½in	Square to axis	90 deg	35 to 45 deg	45 deg	Roughing square section to round spindle
chisel	skew chisel	flat rectangle	¼ to 1½in	½. 1. 1½in	Square, angled		18 to 25 deg	22 deg	Planing cylinders, rounding over, large beads, convex slopes
chisel	skew chisel	long oval	¾ to 1½in	¾. 1. 1½ in	Arc to ½ circ	10 to 80 deg	18 to 25 deg	22 deg	Planing cylinders, rounding over, large beads, convex slopes
parting	beading & parting	square	⅜ to ⅝in	⅜in	Square to axis	90 degrees	20 to 30 deg	25 deg	Sizing and reducing cylinders. Rolling small beads
parting	parting tool, plain	vertical rectangle	standard (⅛in)	Standard	Square to axis	90 degrees	40 to 55 deg.	50 deg	Parting through. Sizing and working depth grooves. Detailing
parting	parting tool, diamond	vertical diamond	standard (⅛in)	Standard	Square to axis	90 degrees	45 to 50 deg	45 deg	Parting through. Sizing and working depth grooves. Detailing
parting	parting tool, wedge	fluted wedge	standard (⅛in)	Standard	Square to axis	90 degrees	45 deg	45 deg	Parting through. Sizing and working depth grooves.
gouge	spindle gouge	shallow double U	⅛ to ¼in	¼. ½. 1in	Square to axis	90 degrees	30 deg	30 deg	Planing concave surfaces
gouge	spindle gouge	shallow double U	⅛ to ¼in	¼. ½. ¾in	Fingernail	0 to 0 deg	30 deg (varbl)	30 deg	Hollowing coves

TOOLS AND EQUIPMENT

As we have now seen, basic spindle turning is not very demanding in terms of tools and equipment; indeed, some of the superb delicate work seen on early furniture was turned on the simplest of lathes using only a few hand-tools. Where spindle turning can become expensive is when you start to mechanize, even automate, some of the spindle-turning tasks that the craftsman still does by hand. Copy devices can be fitted to some standard hobby lathes, but they are not effective. Good copy lathes start at over £8,000, and machines that will cut fancy spirals and flutes are over twice that. Fully automated, hopper-fed lathes for the mass production of banister spindles need a vast throughput of work to justify the huge capital outlay.

The economics are such that many spindle turners using standard and basic equipment can still make a living producing small batch runs for local builders. Fortunately there are some reasonably priced tools and lathe attachments available to the hobbyist and jobbing craftsman that do produce quite good results and speed up some of the basic processes.

In this survey of tools and equipment we will focus only upon the hobby and jobbing craftsman end of the scale; here there are probably five basic areas to think about. First, obviously, there is the lathe; next are the most widely used accessories and lathe fitments; and after this we need to review a range of workshop tools. There are then the special attachments: these we will just identify in this chapter, but we will later examine them in more detail as we consider their use in applying decoration to the basic spindles. Finally there are some particular points and requirements related to health and safety.

THE SPINDLE TURNER'S LATHE

When a beginner asks 'What lathe should I buy?', the only reasonable answer is in reply

Fig. 41 An ideal, small, spindle-turning lathe: a Tyne with a specially made (firm-locking) tool carriage.

to the question: 'Exactly what are you going to turn?' Even the answer 'Spindles!' is not good enough, because we need to know just what sort of spindles and for what purpose; at what level of output; if the lathe will *ever* be used for anything else; and a number of other issues about the spindle turner's aims and intentions.

A spindle, and even a number of different types of spindle, can be turned on a relatively light lathe that will accept pieces of wood of somewhere near 39in (1m) in length and up to 4in (100mm) in width. On this you could make banister spindles, chair legs and the column parts of candlesticks, standard lamps and the like, and as we will consider later, you can even make some longer spindles. If, however, you are going to make items that require discs for bases, then you immediately have quite different lathe specifications, because the maximum radius of disc that the lathe can swing becomes important. Bigger diameter pieces such as table and bed legs also require a much more substantial lathe. If you are to concentrate only on lace bobbins then you will need a well-engineered mini-lathe. Of course, few turners only ever make legs and spindles: most will want to make bases and decorative bosses, and many will want to turn the occasional bowl, or perhaps a few small wheels; some will want to make spinning wheels.

In other words, the average load is going to include both long, thin, between-centres items, but also some broad, face-plate worked, flat pieces. There is therefore no single answer to the 'What lathe?'

Fig. 42 A 1995 Wadkin lathe. This large machine, weighing one ton, has turned a whole holly tree in one go to make a 6ft-long massive candlestick for a stage prop. Now that's spindle turning!

question, because whatever you choose will involve a number of compromises.

The best spindle-turning lathes have a long bed, but the distance between the drive point, the axis of the lathe, and the bed can be relatively small. Face-plate work, on the other hand, requires that you can turn blanks of a much greater diameter; here the distance between drive axis and bed – known as 'the swing over the bed' – has to be much larger.

At one time, the way that lathe design accommodated this problem was to have a normal spacing between drive axis and bed of 6 to 10in (15 to 25cm), but then to have a section of the bed immediately adjacent to the drive head that could be removed. It was known as a 'step bed'. This arrangement was relatively easy to provide in lathes where the beds were of massive cast iron and girder construction, and on some machines allowed the turner to swing a 20in (50cm) plus diameter disc over the bed.

58

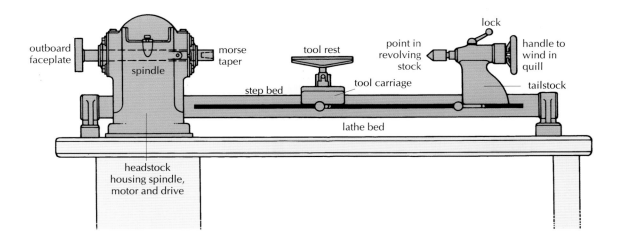

Fig. 43 A modern hobby level lathe.

Many of the light- to medium-sized lathes available today have a bed made of twin steel tubes, and deal with the larger diameters problem in another way. They are made so that the drive head can be swung round, usually through 90 degrees, so that the drive now faces out towards the turner. The tool-rest here is on some cantilever construction or held off the floor in a 'free standing rest'. This is known as 'turning over the front face' and uses a 'swing head'.

Unless you are totally certain that you will never turn anything else but spindles, then a medium-sized lathe with a swing head is the minimum you should consider. Many turners change their first lathe for something bigger and better within a year or two of starting, but a wise, well-thought-through initial choice can render this unnecessary.

Again, pure spindle work does not require the most substantial of machines. You rarely start with a piece of timber that is in any significant way out of balance – and even if you do turn the occasional base, you are likely to be starting with a blank that is already bandsawn to a round. However, flexing and the consequent vibration in long, thin turnings can be a problem; so

some solidity and rigidity in the lathe, its bed and its bench is important.

So forget the basic, cheap, £150 imported lathes, because these are often little more than toys.

As well as size and solid construction, there are many other important things to look at when choosing a lathe. First it should have a good, substantial motor. Some modern lathes have motors which only maintain their rated output by being driven hard and at the limit of their capacity. Three-quarter horse power for spindle turning is the lower limit; 1hp is preferred. So as a base-line the capacity should be 39in (1m) between centres, 4 to 6in (100 to 150mm) over bed (200/300mm swing), 1hp motor, and a swinging or rotating head.

Secondly, the tailstock spindle should be hollow so that a long hole-boring tool can be threaded through it; this is used to drill out the cable ways in standard-lamp columns. Also both the drive spindle and the tailstock spindle *must* have a morse taper so that different drive spurs, points and chucks can be fitted. And the tailstock point *must* be rotating, so avoid fixed points onto which you have to keep dolloping grease –

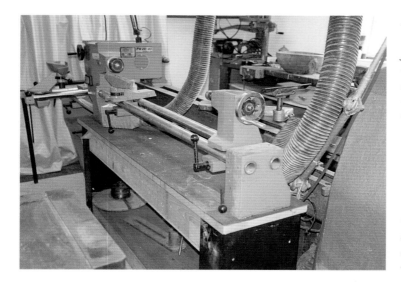

Fig. 44 A Poolewood 28/40. This is my main spindle lathe for which long work steadies, copy fingers and other gadgets have been made. Note the trunking for a piped dust collection system.

(Below) Fig. 45 Drive spindle and tailstock quill have 2MT – size 2 morse tapers – to accept various centres.

these really are a thing of the past requiring, as they do, constant re-adjustment and re-clamping.

Third, it is essential that the tailstock unit and the tool-post can be quickly and easily moved and repositioned. This means that they *must* have handle-adjusted clamps, and should not rely on nuts that require a separate spanner. And it is absolutely essential that while they are readily adjustable, they really do clamp solid: whatever the length of the tool-rest, you should be able clamp it tight so that you can lean hard on the end without it moving in and catching the wood you are turning. And having clamped it this tight, you then need to be able to unclamp it and move it without having to get a monkey wrench.

At one time you had to choose a lathe where the manufacturers also offered a full range of the attachments that you were likely to need; only Coronet, and later Tyne met that criterion. Today it does not matter, as a complete range of non-proprietary attachments are available for almost all lathes from suppliers such as the Axminster Power Tool Company, Craft Supplies and John Boddy, and their various local agencies.

An important thing to watch when choosing a lathe, however – and many of us have been caught out on this one – is that a number of companies are currently selling equipment that has been manufactured abroad. Some sell it under their own international name, and may even *be* the manufacturers. The worst offenders, however, are 'badge engineers', who buy wherever they can, put their own name on it and then sell it. So far no problem! But once the model is withdrawn by the original maker, no spares or replacements are available. I have one lathe under a moderately well known 'badge' name, an angle grinder (and a fishing rod) from another very well known manufacturer/name, and a computer from a major European manufacturer which are all useless for want of simple but totally unavailable spares. When I suggest you should 'buy British', and from a well established, solid company, this is not being nationalistic but merely practical! After-sales service, parts and accessories really *do* matter.

LATHE ACCESSORIES

Again, what you will need will depend upon the type of turning that you are going

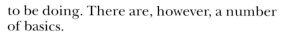

to be doing. There are, however, a number of basics.

TOOL-REST

First must come the tool-rest. The standard with many lathes is somewhere between 6 and 10in (150 and 250mm) long, end to end. This is a good start. Clearly, however, to plane a table leg, 30 to 35in/800 to 900mm long, will mean repositioning the rest five times or so and that really is slow and tedious; so one additional long rest of 20 to 24in (500 to 600mm) length is therefore extremely useful. This will mean two tool carriages, one at each end. It may also mean that you have to have the rest made for you, as many lathe manufacturers do not offer this facility.

LONG WORK-STEADY

You will also need a long work-steady. Turners of old made their own, and one usually consisted of a grooved wooden upright which was mounted to bear on the far side of the spindle so that you were in effect, pushing against it. Modern steadies have three bearings on adjustable arms, set to bear on the spindle and prevent it flexing at all. Some steadies have the bearings mounted around a ring which has to be threaded on over the end of the spindle. Others have an open front face, and these are clearly much more convenient.

Fig. 46 A Klein miniature lathe with a lace-bobbin drive. The long tool-rest is in position. This lathe is used in public demonstrations, hence the safety screen.

DRIVE POINTS

You will need a variety of drive points: cross-head, spur and ring, and these we will consider in a later chapter. We will also look at other drives and chucks, but here we must list a four-jaw chuck, and also a substantial Jacob's chuck on a morse taper drive.

Much of the decoration that you apply to spindles requires that you can locate set points about the radius accurately, and can then hold the spindle in position at these points while you work on it. This will mean some form of indexing head, preferably with forty-eight holes. Some lathes have such a facility built onto the drive pulley, but non-proprietary rings are available for fixing to a number of chucks. Again, we will be looking at the use of such devices later.

HAND TOOLS

We have already identified most of the normal tools that are used for spindle turning, and the table on page 56 shows the tools with the range of profiles, sections and bevel angles that are used on spindles. With the list is an indication of the pieces that make up a basic kit. Included are four **scraper tools**, but it must be said that they are not essential items, since all the jobs that they are used for can be accomplished with the tools we used during the shapes exercise.

What is important is not that you have a huge number of tools in every combination of profile, but that you develop the necessary skills with those you do have. Certainly it is convenient to have a large variety, and also duplicates of some of the most widely used so that you can put your hand on them whenever you need them; but you can end up with a huge investment in tools and the resultant clutter on the lathe bed can be a real hassle.

I would also list amongst my essentials for spindle decoration a small- to medium-sized **power router**. And of course there are a number of pieces of **safety and facilitating equipment** that are required.

The bowl turner requires a large, solid **bandsaw**, though the spindle turner will probably find much more use for a **table saw** and **planer table**. They do not need to be massive, and a small- to medium-sized combination unit stood me in good stead for a number of years. It is useful to be able to produce lengths of a true 4in (10cm) square section, for turning legs; but a table saw with a 3in (7.6cm) cut is often sufficient. The saw table must have a fence to ensure an accurate rip-cut. The saw/planer also need to be sited so that there is a 4ft (1.2m) clearance at either end for handling longer lengths. Of course these comments tend to presuppose that you are only turning spindles. Many spindle turners make furniture, however, and in that case a larger saw table and much bigger planer table are often justified in order to work table tops and carcass elements.

Also, the further you go into furniture-making the more likely you are to find a **morticizer** a very useful addition. However, before your output rises to justify that expense, a **pillar drill** and a set of **morticizing chisel bits** is more than adequate.

You will need **tool-sharpening facilities** and we will also consider what this means later.

The point has already been made that you should not need to use abrasives to clean up a turned spindle, and in fact, the use of sandpaper dulls the crispness of turned detail. However, the process as a whole does create dust and fine chippings, and a good **dust collector** is essential. This needs to be set up with the inlets just behind the main working zone of the lathe. Of course, as you work along the length of a spindle you will need to move the collector input, so flexible trunking is necessary.

And while on safety, don't forget three things. First, a good **first-aid kit**; spindle moulders and planers top the lists for the highest frequency of accidents for any tool used in all crafts and manufacturing industries. Second, you must have a regularly serviced **fire extinguisher** suitable for use on wood-based fires; and third, a **fire blanket**.

I regard personal dust protection as being more important that a dust collector system (and in fact always use both). **Respirator systems** or close-fitting **rubber masks** are essential. Moulded face masks are all right for a short-term visit, but not for a day's work in the workshop.

Clothing generally matters, and there are two considerations: first, you must avoid anything that could catch in rotating machinery; and second, you should try to keep wood dust off the skin. With most woods it does not matter – but some such as iroko, pernambuco, padauk and some rosewoods – are prone to cause rashes. A slip-over-the-head smock in a strong canvas is recommended, and it should have cuffs and a neck-band that can be drawn to a closure. Whether or not you have long hair, a hat is also a good idea.

Recent advances in audiometry have shown that even for the turning operations you should have **ear defenders**, as continuous low-frequency sound 'wears out' the hearing mechanism. They become even more essential once you start using power planers and routers (and chain saws). Furthermore, a lot of turners like music while they work, but so that it can be heard over the noise of the machines the volume is often turned up to a level where it does much more damage to eardrums than does any router or planer. In my own workshop there are four speakers to spread the sound, rather than to have to blast it over long distances.

SAFETY

Your own facilities, the space you have available, and your own style will condition many of your working practices, but there are four general safety aspects to consider.

MACHINES

Make as much use as possible of fixed, static machines that are permanently wired in. Many accidents occur with trailing cables. Power tools are best with short leads, but this means good provision of power sockets. An efficient arrangement is to have the sockets suspended in conduit over the working areas. Keep all tools appropriately earthed, and test the earthing facility at regular intervals.

LIGHTING

The second area of concern is lighting, since accidents are most likely to occur when you cannot see what you are doing. Light up so that there are no dark corners, and provide a good pool of light over and around any machine.

HEATING

Third must be heat. We each have our own preferred level of working temperature, but as a general principle, too much heat makes you drowsy; and you lose too much dexterity and sensitivity if too cold. A number of craftspeople find night storage heaters useful, with hot air blowers as a supplement. Open flame heaters are not recommended – it has been some time since we last heard of an air-dust explosion in a workshop, but it can happen.

STANCE

The fourth, and frequently the least considered safety aspect, is that of stance. The lathe's axis should be at about *your* waist level so that you don't have to bend over the work – and above all, avoid hunched shoulders. Some old turners have had to give up because of fused vertebrae and lifelong back trouble, long before their arthritic hands gave out!

— 6 —

TOOL SHARPENING

Compared with 'proper woodworkers' we turners are slapdash! It has been said of us that 'if it can't be done with a machine, you don't do it – and worst of all, you don't even sharpen your tools properly!' Although in fact when it comes to tool sharpening, we have deliberately worked out our own acceptable compromise. Thus, provided that the tool is at least reasonably sharp and is properly used, the power and speed of the lathe ensure that we achieve an acceptable cut – perhaps not perfect but acceptable!

The way in which turning tools are used – in long bouts of continuous high-speed cutting – blunts them quite quickly: if we sharpened, honed and burnished them on the traditional oilstones, the edges would last a little longer, but we would then be spending most of our working hours at the stone. So we live with the compromise: tools reasonably sharp, a finish that can be lightly sanded to perfection, very quick resharpening; but above all, a reasonable level of output! This we achieve by sharpening on high-speed, coarse-grit, powered grind-wheels, and we use the tool straight off the wheel. Well, almost.

Bench grinders can produce a reasonably flat, even bevel, but they do leave a feather burr on the tool's cutting edge. Although a tool in this state *feels* sharper, it is in fact the burr that we are feeling: remove the jaggedness of the burr and although the edge does not feel as keen, it will actually cut better. So, ideally, after sharpening on the grind-wheel it is best to give the edge a little touch-up on a hand-held stone to remove the burr.

The immediate problem with bench grinders is that the average unit has only a small diameter wheel; this leaves a distinct concave on the bevel which is not ideal for fine cutting, particularly on the skew. A good sharpening grinder should have a wheel of about 8in (20cm) diameter; and the wider the stone, the easier it is to grind an even bevel on a large tool – hence a 1in (25mm) width stone is normally chosen. Most turners opt for sixty- to eighty-grit stones, although some choose finer – even down to 200-grit.

Typical proprietary bench grinders turn at 3,000rpm. This really is unnecessarily fast, and if using an 8in (20cm) wheel, 1,000 to 1,250rpm is quite adequate, provided you only maintain a short contact time to avoid heat build-up.

Few off-the-shelf grinders meet the specification that we are now developing, and for this reason many turners make up their own units with Picador shafts and bearings and old washing-machine motors. Grind-wheels are usually guaranteed to 10,000rpm; 3,000 is one third of that, while washing-machine motors turning at only 1,000rpm are merely 10 per cent of the danger limit. The slower speed not only heats the tool less, it is also intrinsically safer: it is even less likely to burst or fly apart, and the volume of sparks is less – and they are certainly not projected as far (although goggles should still be worn).

Above all, the bench-grinder method is quick, and regularly touching up the tools during a period of turning takes only a few seconds. Wet-stone wheels, and oil- or water-lubricated stones do produce a much

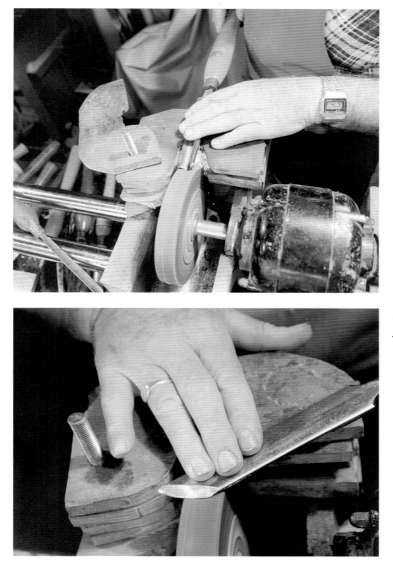

Fig. 47 Sharpening a roughing gouge; the tool is laid flat and is rotated around the blade's axis. The spark guard has been removed to show the action.

Fig. 48 The skew is also laid flat on its platform, but the handle is moved slightly sideways as it is swung through an arc.

better, longer-lasting edge, but they take so much longer to get there; hence our justifiable compromise. We do, however, still use stones to remove the burr after wheel-grinding and to produce a particularly fine edge for a very delicate job, for example the pencil-thin columns of goblets.

The great difficulty in tool-grinding is to obtain the correct bevel angle and one that runs true from side to side of the edge. To achieve this you really need a plate which can be angled to the bevel required, but which allows the tools to lie flat for grinding. Mike O'Donnel has produced an excellent little unit for attaching to a bench grinder; and my own home-made grinder has a series of leaves which work with the tangent of the wheel.

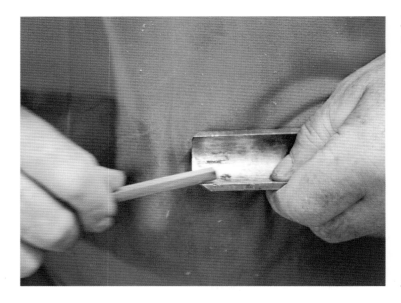

Fig. 49 Cleaning the burr of the cutting edge with a hand-stone.

Fig. 50 Tool bevel angles.

turners have their own favourite angles;
those shown are the basic patterns

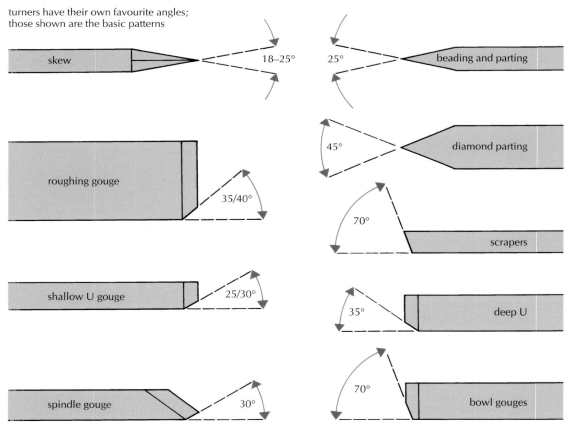

skew   18–25°

beading and parting   25°

diamond parting   45°

roughing gouge   35/40°

scrapers   70°

shallow U gouge   25/30°

deep U   35°

spindle gouge   30°

bowl gouges   70°

Correct sharpening occurs when the table is adjusted to the bevel required, and the tool is placed flat on the table and the bevel rests flat against the surface of the grind-wheel. In this position there will be sparks under the tool, but more significantly there will be a little ripple of sparks on the top of the tip of the cutting edge.

Some are confused by the term 'bevel angle'. This is the angle between the upper and the lower face of the tool across the bevel. Hence a skew (a double-bevel tool) with a bevel angle of 22 degrees will have two bevels, the upper and the lower, each making an angle of 11 degrees with the axis of the tool blade. A single bevel tool such as a U-gouge has only one bevel, and the top of the blade is flat. Hence a gouge of 35-degree bevel has an angle of 35 degrees between bevel and blade axis.

The finer the bevel angle the 'sharper' the tool, and the cleaner it will cut. Skews which are usually used for planing along the grain have a bevel angle of between 18 and 25 degrees, although some tool-makers recommend between 25 and 30 degrees, and beading and parting tools between 20 and 35 degrees. Both square-ended and fingernail gouges are usually about 30 degrees, while scrapers may be anywhere between 40 and 80 degrees – the norm being 70.

A straight-edged skew is held flat on the rest with the handle angled so that the edge lies flat on the stone and parallel to the stone's spindle axis. The blade is then moved from side to side to allow for any slight grooving or unevenness in the stone's surface. Obviously an arc-ground skew is offered up to the stone in a similar way, but once contact is made, the handle of the tool is swung in an arc to radius the cutting edge.

Square-ended gouges are presented at right-angles to the stone and are then merely rotated around the blade's axis. Fingernail gouges on the other hand have to be both rotated and swung in an arc each side of the centre line. All other tools are ground using one or more of these three movements:

1. A straight side-to-side slide;
2. A partial rotation around the blade's axis;
3. A swing of the handle through some level of arc.

When a tool is particularly blunt or has edge damage, more extensive grinding is needed and the blade needs to be dipped into cold water to cool it down after each pass across the grind-wheel.

It is very easy to overheat fine bevel angle tools, and the long point of an arc-ground skew is particularly vulnerable. If a tool does overheat while grinding, a bluing of the steel occurs; this indicates that the temper has been lost, and an edge in this condition will blunt very quickly in use. Blued steel, while not such a problem on high-speed steel tools, should be slowly and carefully ground away with much water cooling.

Of course tools for carving, and particularly the chisels and gouges used in cutting barley twists, need to be sharpened in the conventional way on wet grinders such as the Tormek, or on oil- or water-lubricated stones. Mine get a good sharpening at the end of the day, and the process is as follows: first, profiling on a Tormek; then fine sharpening on a 1,000 and 4,000 Japanese waterstone; and a final polishing on the leather wheel on the Tormek dressed with fine abrasive/polishing compound. This produces a mirror finish on the bevel. With such treatment they will give a good day's work, with only the need for two or three quick stroppings on the leather wheel.

7

HOLDING THE WOOD ON THE LATHE

TIMBER CHOICE

Spindle turners are much more constrained in their choice of timbers than is the bowl turner. Only rarely can we just pick up a nice piece of wood and ask ourselves 'What can I make of this?' Usually we have an item to make and we have to find wood that is specified or is at least suitable for the required end product. Obviously strength and durability are likely to be our first considerations. The fact that many spindles are likely to have to join together or to mate to other wooden elements means that timber variety and moisture content (element compatibility) is also going to be important. There are times when we want particular decoration, and we have to look towards dense, fine-grained timbers. We may occasionally be working with exotics – rosewoods and mahoganies, padauk and others – or with more expensive native woods such as walnut. A lot of work will be in beech and oak, and some probably in pine.

Of course, those working on small decorative items may span the whole range of timbers; for instance, lace bobbin-makers may deliberately set out to find and use as many varieties of timber as possible. Also, collectors of lace bobbins and wooden 'eggs' will usually buy one if it is of a wood variety that they do not already have in their collection.

A lot of what we make will be coloured, stained or painted. A great deal of the 'mahogany' furniture of the Victorian and Edwardian era is actually carefully stained and finished beech.

So here it is probably more appropriate to summarize some of the considerations of timber choice, than to detail all the available materials and their characteristics.

Working with long lengths of relatively small cross-section – the most common spindle-turning feedstock – does reduce the amount of splitting in storage that we have to contend with. If we start with check-free, kiln-dried stock then there should be little problem. The main thing to look out for is that the timber has not been cut from the heartwood, and does not have the actual heart within the cross-section; this is because heartwood can be virtually guaranteed to split as it dries out.

Unless we are making garden dibbers – and they hardly come within the category of decorative spindles – then we are unlikely to be working with green wood. As a starting point we should look to a moisture content of 12 to 15 per cent, this being the UK indoor summer norm. If making furniture for a modern air-conditioned house, however, then the specification could be 8 to 10 per cent.

TIMBER DENSITY

The density of the timber matters in two ways. The more dense it is the more amenable it is to working to fine and crisp detail – hence the more decoration it will sustain. The denser woods are also much more bruise resistant and this can matter with pieces of furniture that are prone to being knocked around or kicked (chair legs and suchlike). For this reason soft, porous timbers such as willow, alder and poplar are rarely used. Softer woods with a long, fibrous grain structure are more difficult to turn cleanly. Larch is one of the worst, and some of the softer pines can be trying!

PIECE DESIGN AND COLOUR

The design of the piece that we are making will, of course, have a strong bearing upon the choice of timber; thus some items of furniture, particularly some period pieces, only look right in oak. The fact that a piece is to be in oak now has implications for the style and detail of the decoration that we use, since oak is not amenable to being worked to crisp and intricate detail. In the same way there is some conceptual incongruity in having broad and relatively crude detail – for instance a raised Tudor rose – on a piece of fine Brazilian mahogany.

If the piece is to be coloured, does the choice of wood really matter? Again, the answer is 'yes'. We still have to choose a wood that will work readily to the level of detail we require, but it must also be suitable for the type of stain or colouring that is to be applied. Thus we rarely want open-pored textures as the supporting canvas for colour except when looking for special effects.

MATERIALS

Of course it will depend upon your level of output, and particularly the amount of copy or repetitive work that you do, but the sourcing of your spindle-turning materials does require some thought. For instance, you need to be turning over a substantial volume of work before buying green timber would become viable, because in this situation you would need a kiln and conversion equipment such as circular saws and heavy duty planers.

As a dedicated hobbyist or a lone craftsman producer you may soon reach the stage where both convenience and economics make it appropriate to buy kiln-dried plank wood from 'wholesale' sources, and then to have a saw and planer of small workshop capacity. This becomes particularly appropriate if you are making a few pieces of furniture each requiring materials of different sizes.

For the rest of us, the economic solution is to work with retail suppliers who can provide consistent quality and variety of squared section timber in the sizes we use most. Unfortunately, only a few such suppliers exist, besides which, many of those in the marketplace offer timber of dubious quality and widely inaccurate moisture content ratings.

Whichever of these categories applies we will also, inevitably, frequently be using wood 'as found': that is, offcuts from various other jobs, 'given' timber, or whatever.

MOUNTING WOOD ON THE LATHE

Looking to the middle road, we must now consider the preparation of wood for mounting on the lathe in or on whatever chuck is appropriate to the task in hand. In this instance, we are talking of feedstock that is in one of three forms: it may be plank wood; or it is already turned to a round; or it is squared – or nearly so.

CENTRE FINDING

The easiest method of centre-finding with four-cornered material (even off-squared stock) is to join the opposite corners with diagonal lines and then to check for minimum radius. With round stock, drawing two lines across the widest diameter at roughly right-angles to each other will provide a centre at the crossing-points.

There are various gadgets available to aid centre-finding. One supplied by Veritas is a plate device which can be screwed to the leg of a workbench or lathe table. This provides a right-angle bracket which has a backing plate with a raised diagonal marking line. The end of the timber blank is couched in the angle plate with the corner of the blank sitting in the angle, and the outboard end of the blank is then struck with a mallet. The raised line indents a diagonal on the base of the timber. The blank is then rotated through 90 degrees and the line is again impressed, and the two diagonal lines cross at the centre. The finder is useful, but it is very easy to mis-align the timber by not getting it flat and tight in the angle, or to get a small build-up of swarf which again mis-places the impressed lines. Even so, this is still a useful gadget provided it is used with care. It also functions well on rounded stock.

Another centre-finding device is a right-angled 'set square' which has a diagonal arm. The square is placed on a corner at the end of the baulk and a pencil line is drawn against the diagonal arm. This is quick and effective on small-section timbers.

The problem with most centre-finding gadgets is that they rely on being used with true square-sectioned stock, and often so-called 'square' stock is not truly such. The vast majority of the items made by spindle turners will be pieces with one or more square-sections, these usually being at the two ends. The bulk of these will be banister spindles and frames, legs, and rails and spacers for items of furniture. It is for this reason that in itemizing the spindle turner's kit, prominence was given to a table saw and a planer.

SQUARING TIMBER

Where you have to produce a spindle that goes from square to round (and possibly back again) it is essential that you start with feedstock (blanks) that are a true square, as it is extremely difficult to square the ends up after turning. Of course, you can produce squared timber by hand – our forefathers did it superbly well – even using pit saws and adzes! Today, however, we just do not have the time.

(Left) *Fig. 51 The Veritas centre-finder. The timber is cradled and the outboard end struck with a mallet. Quick, but care is needed to get a true result.*

Fig. 52 Centre-finding aids.

You can buy short lengths of prepared squared timber, but it is not always easy to find lengths suitable for table legs and rails, and it is a very expensive way of buying timber if you require it in any quantity. So a basic requirement is a power circular saw with a rip-blade and an accurate ripping fence; this is then backed up with a good shooting plane. You will not make many pieces with this set-up, however, before you decide to replace the hand plane with a saw table and a power planer.

PROBLEMS WITH SAW BENCHES

There are three problems with saw benches or tables: first, only 35 to 40 per cent of the blade diameter is available, so for a 4in (10cm) thick table-leg section you need a saw with a blade diameter of at least 10in (25cm). This is a hefty unit which requires a heavy surge current to start it, and it cannot be run off a 13amp plug and socket. Associated with this is the problem that friction increases exponentially with the blade diameter, and while a 10in blade may require only 1½hp, larger circular saws need big motors if they are not to stall and burn out.

The third problem is that of space. As turners, we are used to machines where almost all operations are conducted within the machine's footprint. With saw tables and planers you will need feed and output space outside the ends of the machines' platforms. According to what you are producing you will probably need to put each machine in the middle of a 9ft (2.7m) long clear space.

An essential element on any saw table used for producing squared section is a good ripping fence, and this is where much light workshop machinery falls down. The fence must be absolutely parallel to the face of the blade: if it is only a fraction out of line the timber will pinch, the blade will bind and a burn-out soon follows. Every time you re-set the fence, test for parallel. This is so important that a wise investment is a set of gauge blocks of the sizes to which you most regularly cut. These may be in steel or hardwood.

As turners we become lazy. We are very used to putting our hands or fingers onto the workpiece while it is rotating and unless we are foolish enough to wear loose clothing or bring our knuckles near a jaw chuck, we know that serious injury is unlikely. Saw tables and planers require a level of respect that we are unaccustomed to. *Always* use push sticks, and keep a number of them ready beside the on/off button of the machine – then you won't forget.

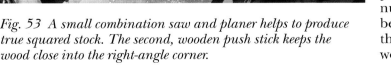

Fig. 53 A small combination saw and planer helps to produce true squared stock. The second, wooden push stick keeps the wood close into the right-angle corner.

Even with the proper machines and cutting fences, getting a true square is not automatic. Start by pushing the timber square against the rip fence, and then, maintaining the sideways pressure, start to feed the timber into the blade. Once a length has gone through it should be held true by the interaction between the riving knife and slight sideways pressure.

PLANERS

Planers and planer thicknessers are in some ways more forgiving – in others they are lethal. The cutting load is much less as there is little or no friction, but the normal speed of rotation can be many times that of a saw and everything therefore happens much more quickly. The key points are first, to ensure that the timber is flat on the bed and is held there with slight downward pressure (using a push stick). Ensure also that it is square on and against the side wall (which should be at a perfect right-angle to the table top). While this downwards and sideways pressure is maintained, the timber is pushed through with a second push stick.

These points may seem laboured, but it is amazing how often an average operator will produce 'square' section that is somewhat rhomboidal! Also, how many woodworkers are short-fingered?

Finally, there are occasions when a table leg is made where the head is of rectangular form. The longest side of the rectangle corresponds to the long side of the table, and the side rail will be mortised into it. In marking off for turning your datum must be the centre axis of the turned part. This may correspond to the centre of the rectangle, but it is more likely to be nearer to one or both outside faces. Draw a square on the rectangular end of the timber to correspond with the axis of the leg, and mount the drive spur to the centre of this square.

'BETWEEN-CENTRES' TURNING

As the name implies, 'between-centres' means that the piece of wood to be turned is held between two mountings, one at either end of the piece. As we recognized earlier, while this is basically true, it is not absolutely so.

Most spindles, of whatever length, are turned whilst being held in position for most of the time at both ends. The drive from the motor has to turn the timber from the drive end, while the piece is held in a fixed axis by some device at the outboard or tailstock end. The simplest means of fixing is between two 'points', positioned so that they are driven into the centre axis of the length of the timber. In all cases the drive end of the timber is either pushed onto some form of 'point', or is held in some form of socket; and it is then held in place by applying pressure from the tailstock point. To achieve this, the tailstock point is mounted in a quill which is threaded into the tailstock block and which can be wound in and out, usually with a wheel handle on the outboard end.

Clearly, if it were a simple point at the drive end it would spin in the timber without turning it. The drive point therefore has to have a means of positively driving the timber, and there are two basic 'positive' means of achieving this: the first is to have the point rising out of the centre of a simple chisel, the wings of which are also driven into the end of the wood; it is these wings that push the timber round. The second and most widely used drive is a development of this, where there are two chisel bits set to form a cross, still with the point in the middle.

FRICTION DRIVES

There are then a number of friction drives. The first is a ring or circular sharp edge

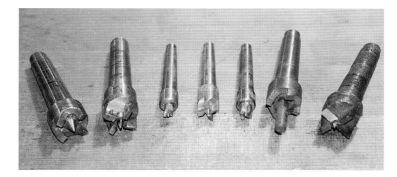

Fig. 54 A set of drive spurs with cross-head chisels and in 1 and 2 MT sizes. One in from the right is the drive for long, hole-drilled columns.

(Below) Fig. 55 A light pull on the special multi-step friction drive.

round the centre point, and is useful where the cross-section of the timber is too small to provide a seat for the chisels. Obviously the ring provides extra friction and this gives drive under light loads.

We then come to a number of friction drive 'points' for special purposes. There is one designed for turning small light pulls and similar, where the blank has a hole drilled into the centre axis, with the diameter of the hole set to a tight fit on a centre dowel on the drive point. Actually the dowel usually has two or three stepped diameters. For light pulls, these correspond to the smaller diameter hole in the pull through which the cord passes, and then a short, larger diameter spigot which accommodates the knot on the end of the pull cord.

A combination drive-point uses a cross-chisel form and a longer dowel centre 'point'. These are used for larger diameter spindles which have been drilled with a cable way, as in the column of a standard lamp.

Another form of friction drive used for spindle- and end-grain turning is the '**cup chuck**'. These have a tapered hole into which the end of a rounded length of timber is driven. As with other between-centres drives, the timber is held in the cup by pressure from the tailstock point.

Earlier it was suggested that turning eggs was good practice; at the time we simply parted them off and finished the ends by

Fig. 56 Friction and other drives. In wood are three plugs for small goblets and suchlike. The cups are for holding eggs so that the ends can be cleaned off. There are three light-pull drives, a square-socket, a lace bobbin drive, and two ring centres.

Fig. 57 A lace bobbin blank in a square-drive socket. The advantage of this positive drive is that minimal tailstock pressure is required on what is a very fragile spindle.

hand. However, cup chucks can be made, into which the eggs are pushed so that after parting they can be mounted in the cup while the ends are turned and polished.

A modification of the cup chuck is a **lace bobbin drive**. In this the aperture is square in section, usually about ½in (12mm) square, and this gives an extremely positive drive to the small, square-section blanks that are used for lace bobbins.

From the basic forms of positive and friction drives, turners develop their own adaptations for special purposes and later we will be looking at particular forms of drive used in off-centre turning.

Passing mention must also be made of the **screw chuck**. Here, a single centre-sited screw is driven into the end of the spindle blank. While these do have uses in spindle

turning they are not widely favoured as it is too difficult to get them perfectly centred down the axis.

To ensure maximum friction with any of the pure friction drives, it requires that there is some pressure exerted by the tailstock point, and this can cause a number of problems. First, undue pressure forces the tailstock point into the timber, which may split.

Second, the greater the pressure exerted by the tailstock, the more likely it is that the wood will bend. If it is a long spindle, the flexing and bending will be greater, and this can be a prime cause of vibration in the fast-revolving timber. A poor, ripple finish is then inevitable.

For this reason, pure friction points are usually only used on small items which are also short in length, for instance, light pulls, lace bobbins, finger tops, wood pen bodies and suchlike. They do have an advantage in that they are very quick and easy to set, and this can be important if you are working on a high-speed production run and do not wish to stop the lathe to change blanks.

The chisel and cross-head points are not totally problem free. First there is the problem of driving them into the end of the timber to give a positive grip. In setting up the earlier sample spindle we first found the centre (and more on this in a minute), then, using a centre punch, we impressed the centre point. The drive point is offered up to the punched mark and is knocked into the timber end until the chisel edges have indented. This is never done by placing the blank against the point on the lathe and then hitting the free end of the wood with a hammer or mallet, because this is a very sure way of damaging the drive spindle bearings.

The safest method is to have a spare drive spur of the pattern that you normally use. Keep this point for impressing the end of the timber before offering it up to the lathe. You can hammer this spur punch into the wood, and it does not matter that in time, the end of the spur will burr over.

It is advisable, however, still to use a plastic or rubber hammer. There is always the problem that if the centre punch, or the indenting spur is hit too hard, there is a real risk of splitting the timber.

Against this there are the difficulties encountered with both very hard and very soft woods. With the hard woods you cannot indent the drive spur too deeply because of the risk of the wood splitting. When you now start turning, it is very easy to apply a little too much tool pressure – particularly during the roughing stage – and the wood starts to spin on the drive spur cutting a shallow circular depression in the timber and losing all drive. With soft wood a different problem arises in that the drive spur acts almost as a drill, sinking deeper and deeper into the drive end. In both cases you have to continually adjust the tailstock during the shaping process.

On very hard woods it is therefore useful to make saw cuts into the diagonal centre-finding lines and to drill a small hole into the centre; the drive spur then sits in the recesses. We still have to consider other options, however.

OTHER OPTIONS

It is here that the screw chuck can be effective: the embossed centre is pre-drilled so that the large screw of a screw chuck can be driven home. This can be a useful drive in the harder woods, but as noted earlier, it does mean that the drill hole must be absolutely true to the axis of the timber, and this is difficult to achieve without a drill jig.

Fig. 58 In hardwoods it is a good idea to make saw cuts to grip the chisels of the drive spur.

Fig. 59 The screw chuck plate fitted to the precision combination chuck from Craft Supplies.

The greatest advantage of all but the cup chucks (and their variants) that we have been considering so far is that the timber blank can be cut to the exact finished length before it is mounted on the lathe, and this means that no timber is lost or wasted. It also means that all measurements for decoration can be laid off from the true ends.

ALTERNATIVE SPINDLE-TURNING TECHNIQUES

Earlier, a passing comment was made to the effect that some spindles may not be turned between centres. Thus there are some turning jobs which are basically spindle-turning operations and which are certainly performed along the length of the grain, but where the outer end of the piece has to be finished free of a tailstock point. In other words the timber has to be held and driven from one end only, and held firmly enough that sideways pressure can be exerted while tooling the length. Again, this may be a job for the screw chuck; it may, on the other hand, be the time that we consider the use of jaw chucks.

All the variants of the jaw chuck have either three or four jaws, the four-jaw type being infinitely more versatile and therefore generally preferred. This is because three-jaw chucks can only be used on timber that is basically round; four-jaw chucks can effectively clamp onto round stock, but may also be used just as effectively on squared timber.

It is worth emphasizing that rectangular or out-of-square timber cannot be securely clamped in any modern jaw chuck.

The wise choice is a four-jaw, 'self-centering' pattern. On these, a single key adjusts all the jaws equally and in synchronization. On older, non-centering models you have to locate the timber as carefully as possible and then adjust each of the jaws separately to clamp the timber. This is obviously very slow and tricky.

For small work, a ½in (13mm) drill chuck – a Jacob's chuck – is an extremely useful three-jaw chuck. You may not even have to purchase one specifically if you have a pillar drill with a morse taper drive shaft. This can be used for holding small-diameter, round material such as dowels, finger tops, gallery spindles and the like. A Jacob's chuck may even be used for lace bobbins although most

Fig. 60 A short spindle held in the robust Axminster four-jaw chuck.

Fig. 61 A finger top being turned using a Jacob's chuck from a drill as the drive head.

turners find a square socketed cup chuck (a lace bobbin drive) to be preferable.

All jaw chucks have limitations. They are not perfect for single end holding against sideways pressure; and it is almost impossible to take a part-worked piece off and then re-mount it exactly on the same centre. Even so, there are several applications where you need to hold a piece firmly from one end only, and goblets and boxes are particular examples.

For short items, a contracting collet gripping a dovetail spigot on the base of the column may be adequate. However, sideways pressure near the outboard end of the piece may test the mounting to the limits. A much more secure mounting is required for longer pieces where sideways pressure against the leverage of the length of the timber will make firm holding essential. The best mount under such circumstances is to use a split ring collet in a groove cut into the waste end of the timber.

The main disadvantage of the split ring collet is that the blank has to be turned to a round first, and then the holding end has to be turned down to a precisely dimensioned spigot that will fit neatly into the collet chuck and the holding ring. The groove for the split collet is a sizing cut into the spigot. This means that there has to be enough length to the spigot first to run on the clamping ring to a point where there is still space to drop the split-ring pieces into the groove. In all, this could mean up to 2in (50mm) of waste wood, and if it is a valuable hardwood this begins to matter.

Many turners use pre-turned spigot blocks which are already sized to fit their collet chucks. The timber blank to be turned is now glued to the outboard end of a block using a liberal quantity of thick-grade Superglue. The turning blank has a very short waste length allowance, possibly ¼in (6mm). When turning is complete, the short waste section is parted through, leaving the spigot block intact and reusable after it has been cleaned up with a simple facing cut.

A good glue mounting will stand considerable strain, although we do not use it

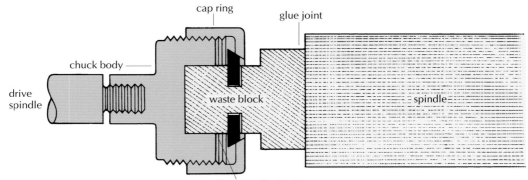

cap ring   glue joint

chuck body

drive
spindle

waste block   spindle

split ring collet (dark)

(Above) *Fig. 62 Section through spindle on glue block held in a split collet chuck.*

Fig. 63 A blank for a goblet mounted on a glue block (thick-grade Superglue) and held in a collet chuck. This will hold firm against any amount of sideways pressure.

unaided. The tailstock point is still brought up to the outboard end and is kept in place while the external profile of the spindle is being worked. The point is withdrawn only while the outboard end is being drilled or hollowed out.

Now you will recall that earlier we said that all work on the outboard end was completed before we started to work down towards the headstock. So in the making of a goblet or candlestick, hollowing out the head is going to be the first thing we do after roughing to a round.

In the hollowing process much of the cutting pressure is along the axis of the column, and this puts little or no strain on the glue mounting. In fact we deliberately try to minimize sideways loading on the inside walls of the hollow.

Once the hollowing is completed, a neat-fitting cap is fitted into the aperture and the tailstock point is now brought up to hold the cap in place and provide extra stability for the whole. Though a neat fit, the cap should not be tapered, nor should the tailstock be wound in hard, as either of these might split the walls of the bowl.

Turners who regularly make goblets and suchlike usually have a box full of preturned caps of various diameters. This mounting arrangement will be seen in action later when we consider off-centre turning. Here, the extra support of the tailstock is vital, as the cutting of the outside profile does impose shock loadings on the glue joint.

Between the items now detailed you can cope with 99 per cent of all spindle-turning mounting problems.

8

DOUBLING THE LENGTH

You can turn spindles of any length irrespective of the between-centres length of your lathe bed, you just make the spindles up in sections. However it is often more convenient if you can make the short to medium spindles (to table-leg length) in one piece.

More convenient? Possibly! More practical? Not necessarily. There is an optimum. In this chapter we are going to be dealing with a number of issues all related to length. Some have a direct bearing upon the choice of lathe most suitable for the type of turning activity that you are interested in; some issues also bear upon the need for special equipment and fittings; and some to particular problems of the inter-relationship between length and diameter. Let us take the easiest one first.

TOOL-REST LENGTH

Most lathes come with relatively short tool-rests, often in the region of 6 to 8in (15 to 20cm) long. Perhaps it is just as well, because many lathes do not have a system of cramping longer tool-rests sufficiently tightly to prevent them moving if leant against. Earlier we were talking about how annoying it is to catch a square corner with the end of a tool-rest because the rest moved. You can understand the manufacturers' dilemma, however: we all want rests that can be cramped up tight so they will not move if we do happen to apply a little pressure or weight; on the other hand, we want to be able to move the rest easily and not have to take a monkey wrench to the handle. The longer the rest the more the

leverage on the ends and the greater the need for a rock-solid clamp. I have to say, very few makers have got it right.

The manufacturers have also gone for another compromise: as so many people turn only bowls, most lathes are now built with bowl-turning in mind. Long rests can be very awkward when you want to work inside a bowl, so the majority of machine makers nowadays provide relatively short rests – far too short to be useful for spindle work. The answer therefore has to be more than one rest, and in fact the solution is probably three or four: one is curved for working inside; one is about a 10 to 12in (25 to 30cm) long for general work; but also one somewhere between two-thirds

Fig. 64 Three tool-rests: short, medium, and heavy duty curved for bowl turning.

and three-quarters of the between-centres length that you most regularly work on. This would mean that you could turn a full-length spindle without having to move the rest from end to end too frequently. Such a rest would certainly have to have two tool-posts and carriages. Many spindle turners buy a second carriage and then get the local blacksmith to make up a rest to order.

OPTIMUM CUTTING SPEEDS

Long thin items give more trouble to spindle turners than practically anything else. Let us recap on some of the basic issues. As stated much earlier, there is an optimum speed for cutting wood with chisel and plane. Planes (assuming that they are nice and sharp) appear to cut best, and be most controllable if passing across the wood at about 25ft (7.5m) per second. Of course, in turning the tool is static and the wood passes across or under the cutting edge – but the principle is the same, and 25ft (7.5m) per second is the optimum to aim for. This means that a spindle of 2in (5cm) in diameter should be rotated at 2,864rpm.

Diameter of Workpiece (in inches)	Required Lathe Speed
6	954
4	1,432
3	1,909
2	2,864
1	5,728
½	11,457

There are not many lathes offering speeds anywhere above 4,500rpm, and lace bobbin makers specializing in ⅜in (10mm) and ½in (13mm) square blanks make their own miniature lathes to get the required speeds. One well known bobbin turner uses a drive that will give him a maximum of 20,000rpm.

THE PROBLEM OF VIBRATION

Any reasonable lathe must run smoothly, but miniature machines have to be precision-engineered if they are to run without intrinsic vibration at 10–15,000rpm. The second problem, also touched on earlier, is the very basic one of between-centres turning. Fundamentally, the spindle is compressed between the two centres, and the greater the compression, the more the wood will bow. Moreover, it takes only a little bowing for the rotating wood to flex and vibrate horribly – the more so the higher the speed of rotation.

Of course if we do not pinch it up tight enough it will bounce within its mounting, and also the drive may fail to grip.

To compound all this, the turner, concentrating on cutting a fine detail or working into a tight corner, can tense up and put a little too much pressure on the rubbing bevel – in fact they bend the wood away from its axis. It only takes a split second and vibration starts, and once it starts, it compounds itself.

Physicists amongst you may be able to work out mathematically the relationship between the length of the spindle, its diameter, the speed of rotation and the amplitude of vibration. At certain critical ratios you reach the natural frequency for the set-up and the spindle behaves as the string on a musical instrument.

If the wood flexes or vibrates at all, from whatever cause, it is at one instant further away from the turner who is carefully keeping their tool edge in contact and therefore tracks the movement. Now the wood flexes backwards and the tool in its forward position bites slightly deeper. In fact you have now created a trough in the surface of the wood and made it out of balance – so the vibration increases, and the slight trough soon becomes a wave form on the surface.

Now the tool tip rises up over the crest of each wave, taking a little off the tip, and then plunges down the wave slope taking an even bigger gouge out of the trough. This ripple finish will get worse and worse until the turner takes positive steps to stop it.

Even the grain on some timbers – with its microscopic hard cores of the long fibres being followed by softer matrix – can be sufficient to get the tool tip bouncing and starting to cut a wave form. And don't forget that flat, thin-section tools can also flex and vibrate.

PREVENTING VIBRATION

There are a number of ways of preventing or minimizing vibration. First, the degree to which the tailstock point is tightened up must be a careful balance between enough tension for the drive to grip, but not enough actually to compress and bend the timber.

Second, the tool must be sharp and applied with a delicate touch. The grasp should be firm enough to prevent the tool being pushed in and out by the grain, but light enough so that you are not pushing down on the bevel and bending the timber.

Third, the edge must be kept to the 45 degrees to the axis to maintain optimum cutting: go to a shallower angle and you start to roll off fibres and create trenches.

If on starting there appears to be any vibration, then try raising the lathe speed. The natural frequency of vibration in any spindle you ever turn is likely to be fairly low. The higher the lathe speed, the further away you are likely to be from any natural frequency or close harmonics.

If it is too late and you have now created a wave or ripple finish, then resharpen the tool, reset the tool-rest as close as possible to the cutting zone, increase the lathe's speed a notch, raise the cutting angle to the axis by 10 degrees or so (to 55 degrees), and go in very gently – take only the tops off the waves. It also sometimes helps to change to another of your skew chisels.

Remember that although you may be starting with a 2in (5cm) square blank for your spindle, once you start turning it you are reducing its rigidity in two ways. By taking the corners off in roughing you have removed a substantial part of its cross-sectional area and, therefore, its strength and inflexibility. Then you start to incise detail – and you may well have a feature where, in the grooves to either side, the finished diameter of the spindle is now only ¾in (19mm).

wave crests created when planing at 45 degrees

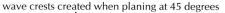

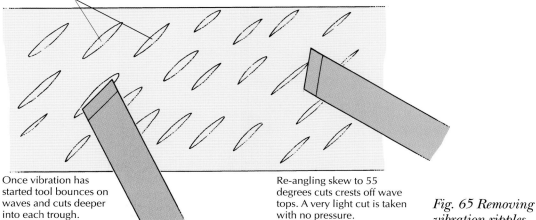

Once vibration has started tool bounces on waves and cuts deeper into each trough.

Re-angling skew to 55 degrees cuts crests off wave tops. A very light cut is taken with no pressure.

Fig. 65 Removing vibration ripples.

Ground Rules when Turning a Decorated Spindle

When turning a decorated spindle there are two ground rules whose application helps to reduce the possibility of vibration. First, arrange the spindle on the lathe so that the smallest diameter part of the taper is to the outboard end; and second, work it in from the tailstock end.

First rough it to a round of equal diameter from end to end (or between the shoulders of any square-to-round junctions), and mark off with a pencil or scriber the locations of key features. Now start on the outermost feature: size it, shape it, and finish it before moving on to the next. One thing that should *not* be done is to cut all the other sizing rings into the round in the middle or towards the driving end of the spindle until you are ready to work on that particular zone. It is tempting to do all the sizing grooves at the same time because it is quicker, but unless you know that the particular piece will stand it, you are risking difficulties that are avoidable.

The Long Work-steady

There is a way of preventing vibration, and this is effectively to halve the length of the spindle being turned. Early turners soon found that when working on thin spindles they could reduce the flexing/vibration tendency by pressing on the rear of the spindle with the index finger of the left hand. When working on fine pieces the thumb of the left hand rests on top of the tool blade and the index finger curls over the piece which is then virtually pinched between tool edge and restraining finger. The problem is that it is easy to friction-burn the finger and to generate substantial callouses.

Long work-steadies replaced the turner's index finger, and go back to the very early days of turning. Originally a piece of wood was fixed to the lathe bed so that it would bear on the back of the spindle somewhere near the half-way point. The face that was actually in contact with the spindle was greased with tallow. Now, even if the turner leant quite heavily onto his tool the spindle could not really bend away from him, and later the bearer was notched to cradle the spindle. Later still the wooden bearer was made adjustable to accommodate different diameters of spindle.

The concept has subsequently been adapted and the notched support was next constructed of two ball-races. Today a ring or semicircle has three adjustable fingers, each fitted with a small ball race at its end. The ring fits round the spindle and the fingers are positioned so that the races bear on the surface of the spindle, firmly holding it in such a way that although it can spin freely it cannot flex at all in any plane.

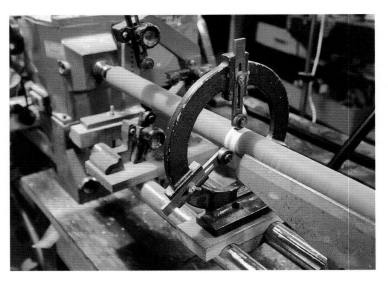

Fig. 66 A long work-steady in position. A running track of masking tape is already in place.

Clearly, where it is positioned reduces the unsupported length of the spindle.

A long work-steady is now an indispensable part of any spindle turner's equipment.

IMPORTANT OPERATIONAL POINTS

There are a few operational points of note. First, the bearings need a flat surface to run on, otherwise they will create a ring mark or angled bruise on the spindle. Second, they can bruise even a flat surface. The answer is to provide a flat ring and then to wrap round three or so turns of masking tape for the bearings to run on. It is sometimes possible that the ring can become a feature in the decoration, although in most cases it will merely be a temporary element which will later be cut away into some design feature. On our earlier spindle the centre bead might well be left as a short cylinder and used as a running track for the long work-steady, in which case the bead would not be finally rounded until all other work on the cylinder had been completed.

This creates another problem: the steady will probably have been positioned somewhere near the centre of the spindle, so when the bearing track is finally worked away, this will be in what is now a vulnerable area of a thinned spindle. Particular care is needed to prevent flexing during this last process – probably using index finger damping.

Long work-steadies have other uses. There are occasions when spindles have to be held at the drive end only (on a screw chuck or in a jaw or collet chuck); this will occur whenever the outboard end is to be drilled or hollowed out, as in forming the socket in a candlestick. A

steady mounted to hold the spindle somewhere near the end provides the necessary stability. Even when a ring tailstock support is used – as when working with a long hole-borer – it is advisable to mount a steady close to the tailstock end to support the spindle.

Most of the long work-steadies normally available are designed to fit a specific lathe. It is, however, usually possible to make up your own metal or wood plates so that they can be adapted to any lathe, and in fact steadies are not difficult to fabricate from scratch.

Obviously, if you are turning pieces of only 1ft (30cm) in length and of 2in (5cm) diameter which will not be thinned down much, then a long steady is not necessary. Even if the 1ft is doubled to 24in (60cm), then a clean job can still be done on blanks that will not be taken below 2in (5cm) in diameter. At 3ft (90cm) in length, however, then the piece is starting to become prone to flexing and requires higher turning skills; and at 4ft (120cm) in length on a 2in diameter spindle, a steady is almost essential. Of course it does depend upon the diameter of some of

Fig. 67 Fitting a Jacob's chuck on a morse taper into the tailstock quill.

the features, particularly those near the middle of the length; thus increasing the base diameter to 3in (7.6cm) and 4ft (1.2m) lengths are no problem.

MAKING AND JOINING SECTIONS

Some turners make four-poster bed legs on lathes of only 40in (1m) clearance between centres; they simply turn the legs in two half-lengths and then join them together. Those with smaller lathes go for three-section legs.

The best means of making and joining sections is by turning a substantial spigot on the end of one length and cutting a socket into the end of the other half. Usually the socket is placed at the top end of the lower section of a composite spindle, and the spigot of the next section is therefore at its base. There is usually something of a bottom-to-top taper in longer-length legs, and the design is worked such that the top of the lower section has an area of larger diameter. This provides a strong casing for the socket. The bottom of the upper section is then turned to a spigot of precise diameter to fit the socket.

DRILLING THE SOCKET AND SPIGOT

Undoubtedly the best method of drilling the socket is to do it on the lathe; in this way the hole will be properly centred, and will be true to that of the lathe and therefore to the leg's axis. Obviously trueness of the joint affects the whole alignment of the spindle.

The difficulty in drilling on the lathe is that of driving the leg element when there is no tailstock point, and where using the drill – probably a large-diameter

Fig. 68 (Above) A long hole auger being fed in through the tailstock quill.
(Right)The auger must be frequently withdrawn for swarf removal; this special point has holes so that the auger does not have to be drawn right out.

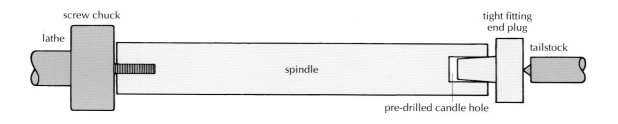

Fig. 69 Supporting a long spindle with a drilled or hollowed end, and plug of waste wood.

saw-tooth bit – as a tailstock would be unlikely to hold the piece steady: the friction load of boring would be too much for the chisel drive point to sustain. The more dense the wood, the greater the probability that the drive would merely spin on the end of the timber.

There are now a number of options, and often you have to make compromises to suit the equipment that you have. It is possible to use a screw chuck to drive the leg, and to position the stabilizing long worksteady somewhere along the spindle (as near to the outboard end as the decoration design will allow). More reliable, however, is to provide for a length of waste wood at the drive end, and to grip this in a jaw chuck while drilling (again using a steady for stability); the final stage being to part away the waste.

If you have a drilling jig, or are particularly accurate with a hand-drill, you may be able to bypass all these more complicated options. Start with the square blank, find the centre, and then drill the spigot hole of the diameter required into what will be the outboard end. Now mount on the lathe a scrap of wood which is about an inch longer than the spigot hole and of just over the spigot diameter. Turn this into a slightly tapered plug that fits snugly into the drilled hole. Fit the plug into the spigot

hole and mount the main blank onto the lathe. The centre mark for turning the plug will now provide the indent for the tailstock point as the leg section is mounted for turning.

THREADING A JOINT

A couple of centuries ago the idea of joining lengths of a composite spindle with spigot, socket and glue would have been anathema to a self-respecting craftsman: he would have threaded the joint. Few now make tapped and threaded joints, but screw threads are still used for special purposes such as the tensioners on spinning wheels.

Special taps and dies are available for threading woods, but it has to be said that only the more expensive are worth buying. The cheaper models do not cut cleanly and the edges dull quickly; furthermore the basic taps will often not cut down to the bottom of a socket, and a second, bottoming tap, is then required.

You also need good saw-toothed bits to pre-drill for threading. The instructions for the various makes of tap and die sets differ a little, but in most cases the hole for the spigot is drilled ¼in (6mm) less that the finished size, while the spigot to be threaded is made ¼in oversize. This allows for a thread amplitude of ⅛in (3mm) and a snug fit.

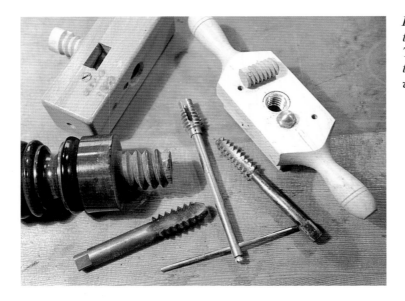

Fig. 70 Tap and die sets for threading spindles and sockets. The old square piano leg has a threaded spigot. Not all woods will support a reliable thread.

As with all drilling operations into wood, the tap has to be withdrawn frequently for swarf removal; this also tends to ease the joint slightly. Some users recommend the use of a little French chalk to lubricate the passage of the tap, and certainly a little chalk helps on the finished thread.

Not all woods lend themselves to threading; for instance, only the very largest diameters and coarse pitch threads are acceptable on oak. Beech, mahogany, apple, cherry and yew cut nicely, but the cutter has to be very sharp for yew. Some rosewoods are excellent and box will take threads of near machine pitches. Some of the more dense pines are alright, although in general it has to be said that pine and walnut are not ideal threading woods. There are two aspects of the good/poor problem: one is that the timber must have a sufficiently fine grain so there is a reasonably low friction between the threads (greatly helped by the application of French chalk); and the other is that the density of the timber must be such that the threads themselves will not break off along the grain.

DRILLING HOLES

There are two basic types of hole that we drill into the ends of spindles: one is the socket into which something is to be fitted – the spigot of the next section (which may or may not be screw threaded), a candle or a light-bulb holder; the other is a long, 'through-hole' for something to pass through – the cord of a light pull, or the flex for a lamp.

As suggested a few moments ago, any drilling operation puts a substantial load on the drive. To keep this loading to a minimum we do three things: first, the lathe is turned at the slowest possible speed; secondly the drill, of whatever type is used, is frequently withdrawn so that swarf can be removed; and of course the bit is frequently resharpened. When turning green woods you must be obsessive about swarf clearance otherwise it will build up behind the drill head, and with the heat generated by drilling it will fuse into a solid mass; this then has to be gouged out before the drill can be withdrawn.

The friction build-up can also be considerable, so again, there are times when you drill, withdraw, allow a cooling period, and then drill a little further. Do not let the drill cool while still down the hole: the head of the bit may contract on cooling, but the swarf ring will solidify.

You very quickly learn one thing when you start drilling large diameter holes, and that is how wet the wood is, particularly some of the imported exotics. You may well have bought it as 'part seasoned', but sap will bubble out and volumes of steam will condense on the tailstock unit.

SMALL DRILL HOLES

For small drill holes – as for lamp pull-cords – ordinary machine twist drills are satisfactory. For sizes up to ⅜in (9mm) wood augers can be used, but auger fluting cannot cope with the waste removal required by large-diameter bits, even at the slowest speeds that the lathe is capable of. For anything larger, saw-tooth drill heads are essential. Some turners use very frequently resharpened spade bits, but these are not recommended for lathe drilling.

All of the bits so far identified can be held in a Jacob's chuck fitted with a morse drive taper suitable for the tail- (or head-) stock of the lathe you are using. With the lathe turning slowly and the chuck and bit in the tailstock, the quill can be advanced to cut clean accurate holes into the end grain of any type of wood.

LONG THROUGH-HOLES

The second type of hole – the long, through holes – do create a number of equipment requirements. Long shell augers – a bit with a single scoop, fluted auger head on the end of a long rod – are made for the purpose; but the lathes on which they can be used are limited. The lathe must have a hollow tail-stock spindle, and either have a tailstock from which the point itself can be removed, or you will need to obtain a special hollow centre. (There is no difficulty here as these can be obtained at most craft suppliers.) It is important however to check on the size of auger that your lathe will accept. Augers are usually available in ¼in, ⁵⁄₁₆in and ⅜in (6mm, 8mm, and 9mm) diameters and of between 24 and 30in length. To exemplify, my huge Wadkin lathe does not have a hollow spindle at all, and even the big Poolewood 28/40 will only accept the medium-sized ⁵⁄₁₆in (8mm) auger.

Again, the secret of use is slow lathe speeds and frequent removal of the tool for swarf clearance; but there is now one more element. If you apply too much pressure to push the tool in, you may cause it to deviate from the centre line. Although the turning motion of the wood around the drill will provide a centralizing tendency, it is still possible for the auger to wander.

When drilling 'through'-holes it is important to measure accurately the length of

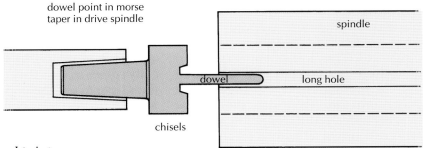

dowel point in morse taper in drive spindle

spindle

dowel

long hole

chisels

Fig. 71 Using a dowel point for long hole work.

87

penetration required and to mark off the shaft of the auger to an appropriate depth. Otherwise it is possible to drill through the length of the spindle and for there to be contact between the auger point and the point of the drive – one will drill away the other! Stop just short and finish by hand.

There are, however, special drive points to deal with such problems. Dowel points have a conventional cross-chisel head, but in the centre of the cross the point has been replaced by a dowel of some 2in (5cm) in length. They are available with dowels of ⁵⁄₁₆ and ⅜in (8 and 9mm) diameter, and can be used in either of two ways. The normal and preferred method is to mount the spindle on conventional centres using a long work-steady, and to shape and finish it before setting up the long hole boring equipment. Auger the spindle to a little over half-way down its length. Withdraw the auger, dismount the spindle, and replace the standard cross-head in the drive stock with the dowel cross-point. Now turn the spindle round so that the part-augered hole fits over the dowel (having indented the end with your old cross-head punch). Refit the tailstock ring, and now auger the remaining half of the hole.

The alternative is quicker, but less reliable. Here you indent the drive end with a cross-punch, and then drill a deep hole of the correct diameter for the dowel drive into the centre of the end of the timber. Now mount the spindle on the lathe and auger normally. This time the auger has to be pushed through the spindle until it meets the hole drilled for the dowel. It is not as good as the double-ended method because there is a considerably increased friction in driving the long auger right through, and there is always the risk of some drift. Indeed, with some longer spindles you may not be able to get right down the length of the spindle with the auger, so you have to do a double-ender!

MAKING IDENTICAL FEATURES

The last of the special long-work mounting and turning problems to be addressed here is the making of identical features. Quite often turned elements are used for decoration purposes on pieces of furniture, and frequently these are arranged either side of some feature. Most commonly they are to be seen framing the sides of the face on long-case clocks, and sometimes ornamenting the side frames of cupboard doors on period sideboards. There are times in these situations where the turned elements used are free-standing columns or mini-pillars. These are turned between centres as are any other spindles, but of course the need for accuracy in copying is paramount. With table legs a minor difference is lost, but it is blatantly obvious in two columns either side of a clock face.

SPLIT TURNINGS

It was probably to deal with this problem that in the past many designers started to use split turnings. If a single spindle is halved down its length then the two elements are bound to be identical. If you are a genius with a fine bandsaw you may be able to halve a spindle cleanly end to end – however, the normal way of producing split turnings is to join two pieces of timber together temporarily, turn them as one, and then separate the two halves again. Obviously to get two even halves the joint has to be down the central axis. That in itself is no problem. The difficulty comes in that having joined them, you then have to get them apart again once the turning process has been completed.

How you do this depends primarily on the length and, to a lesser extent, on the finished diameter of the piece. Let us consider the problems each method presents.

Fig. 72 Two half timbers are spot glued together for split turning. The main hotmelt glue zones are in the two waste ends, and these will be cut away to aid separation.

THE MAIN PROBLEMS

First the main problems. If you use glue and apply this down most of the length, and the spindle is fairly small in diameter, it is probable that in trying to pull them apart one or both will snap. So the first alternative is to use glue, but only a few dabs at critical points. If it is a hot-melt glue you can then separate the halves fairly easily with a hot knife-blade. Alternatively, animal glues may be separated with steam and a knife-blade.

There are times when all you need to glue is the two ends, and these are much easier to get apart. But if the centre of the spindle is taken to a fine diameter there will be an increased tendency to flexing and vibration if the halves are not also held together somewhere near their centres.

Fig. 73 (Above) The split turning completed. The two outboard waste ends with the main glue blobs will be cut away to aid separation . (Right)The two halves are eased apart with a hot knife.

THE MAIN SOLUTIONS

An old face-plate chucking method is a useful approach – it is known as the 'glue sandwich'. Here, the two halves are glued together at key points, but a layer of soft card or thick, fibrous paper is glued between them. With this method the two halves can be pulled apart fairly easily as the card tears through. The glue and card waste is then cleaned off the now opened face.

You can reduce the amount of glue used by adapting the way that the jointed block is mounted on the lathe. As the glue joint is down the centre axis, this means that the point of the cross-head and the tailstock point are both working into the joint trying to force it apart. This requires that you have a particularly good joint at either end.

There are now two things that you can do. One is to use a cross-head drive point, but to set the point so that it does not protrude very far. You also impress it so that the wings of the cross are diagonal to the joint seam. At the tailstock end use a ring centre instead of a point.

The other alternative – and this can be used in combination with any of the foregoing – is to use a blank that is longer than the required spindle length. Heavily glue – even screw together – the two ends which are in the waste zones; eventually the glued/screwed waste ends are cut away and discarded.

My own preferred method is the waste block approach using hot-melt glue. A good dollop of glue is applied to each end and then a blob at the centre. The piece is immediately clamped in a vice which is wound tight to squeeze the glue – it is much harder to get a good finish if there is any gap between the two halves in the turned zone. When the turning is complete, the waste is cut away, hopefully revealing an unglued joint. The two halves are then gently prized apart with a hot knife through the central glue blob.

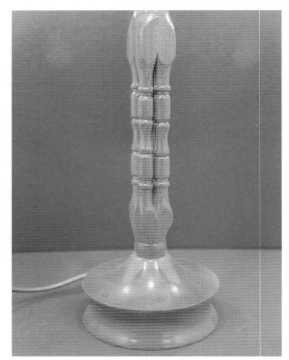

Fig. 74 Four identical spindles with square ends are glued together and then re-turned to finish the ends. (Courtesy Ian Durrant)

Now for two specials: one is attributed to Ian Durrant (of whom more later); the other, also used by Ian, is much older. The old idea is quite simple: four spindles are turned, each identical to the other, and each having square-to-round ends of the same size. After turning, the four are glued together in the square-ended sections to form a four-column split turning. The ends of the composite may be left square, or may themselves now be turned to a round. This arrangement is particularly effective on larger table lampstands.

Ian's special is the ultimate test, and a supreme example of drilling out – hence the brief reference to it here, since the details will be given later in the chapter on spirals. It is most impressive!

9

AN INSIDE EDGE

Although most of our work on spindles so far has been on the outside, we have made a small excursion into the inside of the spindle when talking about the making of spigot, candlestick and cable holes using drills and augers. Now we need to go a little further.

We also need to look briefly at face-plate turning, as many of the spindle items we make require face-plate-turned bases. This involves the use of deep U-bowl gouges, although usually only the medium and smaller patterns.

MAKING BASE PLATES

The making of base plates is the simplest end of face-plate turning, and there is certainly no need to complicate the process here. First the piece of timber has to be mounted onto the lathe, and we can do this quite effectively with the equipment we have already examined.

Start with a disc that has been bandsawn to an approximate circle; with these larger cross-sectional area discs, roughing to a round from square timber is not really practical. The disc can be mounted on the lathe in a number of ways, and the procedure will vary depending upon what you are doing. Let us consider some of the alternatives.

With almost every base you make you will wish to work both of its sides. In most cases you will have a spigot hole to drill and some profiling to do on the upper face, and a rounding and smoothing on the underside. This means that you will need to mount the disc twice so that each face can be worked.

WORKING THE UNDERSIDE

It is usual to work the underside first. To do this the upper face may be screwed to a face-plate or mounted on a screw chuck. If using a face-plate, then short screws are used, positioned in zones that are to be cut away in later profiling. A screw chuck may be driven into the central area; later it will be taken out as the spigot hole. There is a third alternative, and this is to glue on a mounting block for clamping onto a screw, or into a jaw or collet chuck (the block is then cut away when the top is profiled). There are times when you may wish to have a glue block on both faces of the disc. Hot-melt glue or Superglue are ideal bonding agents for this job.

With the disc mounted on the lathe and the eventual underside of the base showing, the outer edge of the disc is turned to a round and the base is trued and cleaned. At this time you also prepare for the second mounting. This may involve the cutting of a recess for a dovetail collet, but it is often easier to glue another block of wood to the centre of the underside of the disc. Hold this in place with the point of the tailstock while the glue sets and at the same time turn the block so that it is round and true to the centre. This truing enables you to later hold the block in a jaw chuck or to prepare it for fixing in a collet. Once the base is cleaned and the mounting block shaped and centred, turn the disc round.

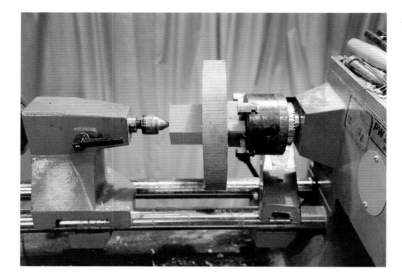

Fig. 75 A lamp base disc with two glue blocks so that both upper face and underside can be turned. Usually the base block is only glued on after the disc has been rounded, the base cleaned and the edge shaped.

WORKING THE TOP FACE AND REVERSE CHUCKING

The top face is now worked and the whole is finished and polished. The final stage is to remove the second (the underside) glue block, and this can often be done by a sharp blow with a mallet. The glue is cleaned away and any roughness removed by hand sanding and polishing. The alternative is to remount the base, base outwards. and to turn the wood block away. However, this clearly requires a homemade wooden face-plate with grooves cut into to hold the base in place. This third mounting is what is known as 'reverse chucking' and is widely used in bowl-turning circles to remove tell-tale chuck marks from the underside of bowls.

TOOLS AND TECHNIQUES

The work on the faces of bases is done with a small size bowl gouge. This deep U-profiled tool is used to shear-cut across the face, the direction of cut being dictated by our rule of always cutting downhill. Hence, because the disc will have grain running across the face plate, it means that a base with the usual dome centre will be cut from the centre out to the rim; whereas a concave dish will be cut from the rim towards the centre.

The bowl gouge cuts with the bevel rubbing and with the cut half-way up the trailing edge of the U. The open top of the U leads by facing two o'clock. This means that, in effect, the actual part of the edge that is cutting is at about 45 degrees to the radial axis of the disc, so you now get a 'shear' cut very similar to that achieved when skew planing.

To achieve true flatness of the underside, the gouge makes most cuts from the rim in towards the centre; but it is then useful to roll the gouge over and draw it back from centre to the rim for the final pass. Normally your eye will tell you whether it is a true flat or slightly concave, but if in doubt test with a square edge. Obviously you must not have a convex (rocking) base!

Most top profiles will be composed of concave and convex curves. Occasionally, however, there will be steps and square-edge sections. You cannot (easily) make facing cuts into a face-plate disc using a

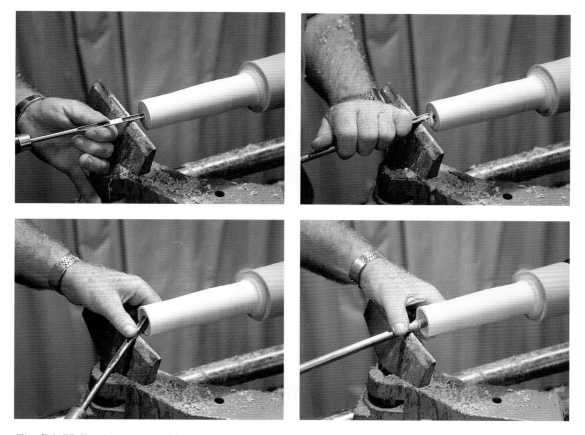

Fig. 76 Hollowing out a goblet.
(Top left) The depth to be hollowed is fixed by pushing a spindle
gouge down the centre axis. The masking tape sets the depth.
(Top right) The bowl of the goblet is hollowed working in towards
the depth hole.
(Bottom left) As the hollow develops the gouge is angled to shear-cut
the walls.
(Bottom right) A goblet scraper is used to clean up the curves.

skew point, and it is here that you may have to resort to scrapers.

'Scraper' is a misnomer: scrapers are still cutting tools, and provided they are correctly sharpened, they should be used to take light cuts and not to tear away chunks of wood. They are used with the tool-rest at just below axis height, and the tip of the tool angled slightly downwards. Scraper cutting-edges are ground to various profiles to suit different jobs.

Scrapers also have to be used for some jobs in hollowing out.

To make a true, vertical hole for a candle in a candlestick, the best method is to use a saw-tooth bit. However, it is a good idea to then relieve the hole with a slight taper, and this is done with a side-cutting scraper.

MAKING LARGE DIAMETER, DEEP HOLES

When you wish to make larger diameter deeper holes, as in goblets and the inside of boxes, then most of the work is still done with small bowl gouges. Deep, right-angled inside corners however are then cleaned out with a diamond side-cutting scraper; this has edges ground on the end and down one side, but the corner is a few degrees under the right-angle.

HOLLOWING OUT

The first step in hollowing out with a gouge is to drill a central hole to the depth you require. This may be done with the lathe stopped using an auger bit in a drill or brace; alternatively it may be drilled with the lathe running and using a machine bit in a holder. The easiest method, however, is to use a small U-spindle gouge, which is simply pushed straight into the centre axis of the rotating wood. The machine bit or gouge is held on the top of the tool-rest which is set at half the tool's diameter below the axis height. Whichever method you use, it is advisable to wrap a little masking tape around the bit or shaft to indicate the exact depth you wish to achieve.

With the centre depth established, you then enlarge the hole with the small bowl gouge. Each cut starts a little further from the centre and penetrates a little deeper in towards the base. It is a series of scooping cuts. This continues until the required interior profile is achieved or until the depth/top aperture ratio is such that the edge of the tool can no longer be kept in cutting contact. At this stage you may have to opt for a gouge with a shallower bevel angle, or turn to a side-cutting scraper of suitable profile.

Fig. 77 A selection of scrapers. The big domed scraper may be used on straight spindles, and the diamond side-scrapers come in handy for cleaning out the inside corners of boxes. Normal scrapers are rarely used in spindle turning.

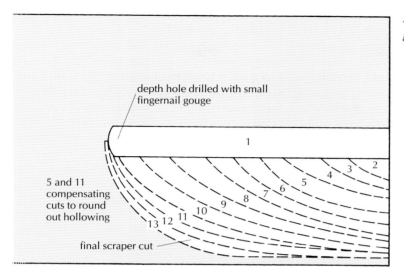

Fig. 78 Hollowing out a goblet bowl – cuts sequence.

In turning bowls you normally establish the external profile first and then hollow out the inside to a matching profile. In making goblets you work in reverse, and profile and finish the inside before starting to work on the outside. We saw the reason for this when turning long spindles, and emphasized the need to work inwards from the outboard end.

With a goblet you have a wide bowl, and then quickly narrow down to a much thinner stem. You cannot work outboard of the smaller diameter stem once you have shaped that, because the piece wouldn't just vibrate – it would snap!

WORKING THE EXTERNAL PROFILE

Once the bowl has been hollowed it is a good idea to make a small cap to fit into the top, and then to bring up the tailstock point to bear on the cap. Do not put any pressure on the point, however, or again you are likely to snap the stem when you fine it down. The support of the tailstock point is particularly useful while exerting sideways pressure as the outer wall is worked. Of course, while developing the external profile of the bowl

you will need to remove the plug at regular intervals to check that you are not making the walls too thick or thin.

There are many times when working on a goblet that you will wish to provide support to the area being cut. Frequently you will be working with the tool in your right hand and the grip just behind the end ferrule. (I also have the right index finger pointing outwards and lying on the top of the tool blade for extra stability and control.) The thumb of the left hand is on the top of the blade of the tool to steady and position the cutting tip. The left index finger is curled round over the top of the rotating workpiece to 'pull' the wood onto the tool's edge; this helps to control the cut, it supports any thin section of the work, and damps out any tendency to flexing and vibration.

MAKING BOXES

The making of boxes is really a subject in its own right; however, as we have already dealt indirectly with most of the tooling aspects, we may as well briefly round the subject out to a conclusion.

Here the sequence of development is normally outside, inside, outside. Boxes are usually mounted on the lathe in a similar manner to goblets. This means shaping the base of the wood to fit into a collet chuck, or gluing to a waste block which is so shaped. It is important that the mounting is secure, and that it doesn't require any additional support from a tailstock, as there is a stage in the working – when the lid is parted off – when there is a much greater sideways loading applied than there is at any stage of the working of a goblet.

MAKING AND FITTING THE LID

The approaches used by different box-makers vary to an extent, and a lot depends upon what they wish to do with the inside of the lid. Basically the blank is first roughed to a round and then the outside profile is worked – including, in most cases, the shaping of the top of the lid.

The lid is now parted off and the box is hollowed out, and the lid is then pushed back into place while the whole is sanded and polished. If the lid itself is to be hollowed or undercut in any way it usually means not finishing off the top profiling but leaving a section of waste wood on the outboard end (the top); this may then be gripped in a jaw chuck.

The parting of the lid from the body is carried out with the thinnest possible parting tool. Two cuts are made: the first is a shallow cut to form the spigot on the bottom of the lid; the second is inboard of this (and possibly slightly overlapping), and this is taken right through to part off the top section.

There are two approaches to fitting the lid into the body: one is for there to be a small indent into the top of the rim of the body, and for the lid spigot to fit into this; the second is for the spigot to be of the full diameter of the hollow in the box. The box is hollowed – with or without a step in the inner rim – so that the lid is a snug fit. A well made box is one where there is a slight 'plop' of inrushing air when the lid is removed.

CLEANING OUT THE INSIDE

Unlike goblets, boxes usually have a right-angle corner deep inside where the walls meet the base. This can only be produced with a scraper, and the ideal tool to use is a diamond side-cutting scraper; this has a square end to the cutting edge, but it is also ground to cut along the side of the blade.

Fig. 79 The bowl is finished first and an end plug is then fitted to provide tailstock support while the outer surface and then the stem is cut. The index finger provides anti-flexing support by pressing against the force of the beading and parting tool planing the stem.

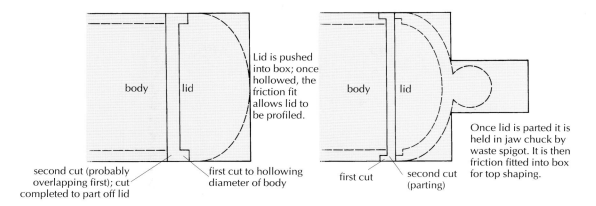

Fig. 80 Parting off box lids. (Left) Spigot left on lid. (Right) The interior of the lid has to be worked while gripped from the waste block.

FINISHING OFF

Once hollowing is complete and the interior cleaned out and finished, the lid is put in place. Try to get the best possible alignment of the figure on the lid with that on the body of the box (you will have lost a little in cutting the parting and spigot slots). Push the lid home, restart the lathe and finally finish the outside of the box.

If a waste piece was left on the lid top, this may now be turned away. If you did not get the dimensioning quite right and the lid is a little loose, it may be held in place with a lap of masking tape while the waste is cut away – but try to do better next time!

CONCLUSION

The notes here cover the basic mechanics of box and goblet turning; the process of cutting the wood is substantially the same as for profiling the length of the faces of spindles. There is one key difference, however, and that is, the moment you start hollowing out you are working into end grain. In fact this is no problem, because provided you keep the tool sharp, end grain will often cut more cleanly on the same piece of wood than will working across the grain. Timber removal is much slower, however.

CUTTING CAPTIVE RINGS

Before leaving goblets there is one fancy addition to be mentioned: you will sometimes see goblets with a captive ring on the stem. Of course similar rings appear on other items – they are an almost essential element on a wooden rattle, and they provide a particular enhancement to Dave Register's wondrous trunnion boxes.

Dave grinds his own tools for cutting his neat and often tiny rings, and now Sorby's have produced a three-piece tool kit for the purpose. First there is a bead-cutting tool as described elsewhere in this text; but there are then a right- and a left-handed semicircular scraper for cutting the rings away from the spindle. These work very well, but are limited in that the size of ring they will cut is governed to a large extent by the fixed radius of the beading tool and the size of the semicircular scrapers.

10

MORE THAN ONE

How uninteresting it would be if spindles only ever came in sets of one. To me the most exciting, challenging and rewarding aspects of all forms of turning is the reproducing of a number of identical spindles. Yet how dull and demotivating is the phrase normally used to describe this activity: 'copy turning'! It is claimed that there are machines that will do this for you, but I have yet to find one – at least one that I could afford! Before manufacturers take the hatchet to me, let me explain.

There are copy machines that do an excellent job – the problem is that they cost almost as much as it does to breed, educate, feed and then train a good copy turner – many, many thousands of pounds. The machines will reproduce good crisp detail, and they will dress the spindle to a fine finish. Most in this category use routers or power-driven cutters, and the only limitation on the complexity of the pattern that they will cut is the availability of suitable router bits or cutting heads. These machines are big, they are usually computer controlled, fully automatic, and with the top end of the range, you just feed an armful of blanks in at one end and collect bins full of finished spindles at the other.

One of the leading names in this field is a company that markets a wide range of superb German-made copy lathes: Hapfo

Fig. 81 This gate-leg table has eight legs which must have identical profiles.

Pollards Ltd, based in Milton Keynes. Looking through a Hapfo catalogue you will see a continuum of lathes which as they increase in simplicity so they fall in price until you are in the £8–10,000 bracket. The trouble is that the simpler they are, the less crisp is the finish they produce, and the less complex the designs they will reproduce. The top end of the Hapfo range is a machine that will cut a twist on a column 13ft (4m) in length and 24in (600mm) in diameter. There are also machines that will deliver a high rate of hollow twists and even 'square turnings'.

So, yes! there *are* good copy lathes; it is at the other end of the scale/price range that things come adrift. Here there are copy devices which mount onto standard hobbyist/craftsmen lathes, but even the best of

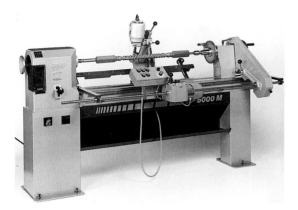

Fig. 82 The Hapfo 5000 programmable copy lathe showing a powered router cutting-head.

these turn out only indifferent work. What is more, the setting-up, and then the 'touching up', and finally the cleaning of the mess they produce, often requires more time than is needed to produce a small run of copies by hand. The problem with anything but the very large router cutting lathes is that all the rest reproduce the profiles with scrapers (usually tungsten carbide-tipped lathe tools), and even with new or newly sharp-ened cutters, the finish they leave is rough. Also they will not cut into sharp corners, nor cut clean vee-grooves. So after rough turn-ing on the simpler copiers the spindles have to be hand-finished: the surfaces need

Fig. 83 A typical copy attachment on a hobby lathe. The cutter is a simple tungsten carbide scraper tip.

Fig. 84 The worst example! The crude detail and the torn surface produced by a typical copy attachment. Using pine timber gives the worst results.

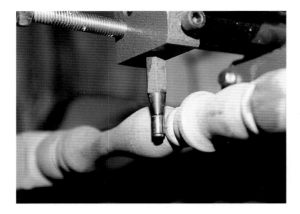

Fig. 85 The finger that traces the profile cannot probe deep grooves nor track vertical faces.

planing, corners and detail need finely shaping, and the whole piece will need sanding.

HOW THEY WORK

Outside computer-controlled, design-programmable, automatic machines and their close relatives, most copiers work on the principle of using a finger or stylus to track along a profile. This in turn articulates the tool carriage, which controls the movement and penetration of the cutting tip. The profiles can be in one of two forms: one uses a finished spindle of the size and pattern being produced; and the other has a template profile of the design, and the stylus traces the outline of the template. Usually the finger is a small-diameter ball bearing, and obviously it is the size of this bearing that determines how deep it will trace into a notch or groove. Clearly it cannot trace into a right-angled corner, nor will these devices produce vertical facing cuts.

It must again be emphasized that these cautionary comments apply specifically to copy lathes and copy attachments using lathe bits as scrapers. In view of the success of machines using powered cutters, there is clearly scope for the craftsman to experiment with fitting a router to a lathe to produce both intricate decoration and even small runs of copies.

COPYING BY HAND AND EYE

At the end of the day the more skilful craftsmen find that, on a combined speed, price and quality calculation they can beat many copy lathes and any copy attachments in producing small runs using hand and eye and ordinary hand tools only. Let us therefore consider some of the methods they use.

First, the required spindle should be drawn out, ideally to full size. This is then measured off, and a spindle is turned to the required dimensions; in making this first spindle any needed design modifications can be made and any fine detailing added, and this now becomes the pattern. From here, a number of routes can be followed, though we are going to examine three of them. We might call them the freehand method; the measured-off method; and 'copy fingers'. Each has variants.

THE FREEHAND METHOD

The freehand is used by some highly skilled professionals. In its simplest form, the pattern spindle is turned and then placed on the lathe bed, and the dimensions are transferred to each new blank as it is mounted merely by eyeing up the pattern and making a few guide marks on the roughed blank using a pencil or scriber. Clearly the copies are never identical, but with the most skilled turner the differences are just enough to indicate that the pieces are hand done, but are always sufficiently similar to be wholly acceptable.

A minor sophistication of the eyeing-up approach is to have a strip of lath or ply into which nails are hammered, and driven

Fig. 86 Methods of marking out for copying.

A layout board for a table. Dimensions of all elements are drawn out full size. It is used as a marking/laying out template.

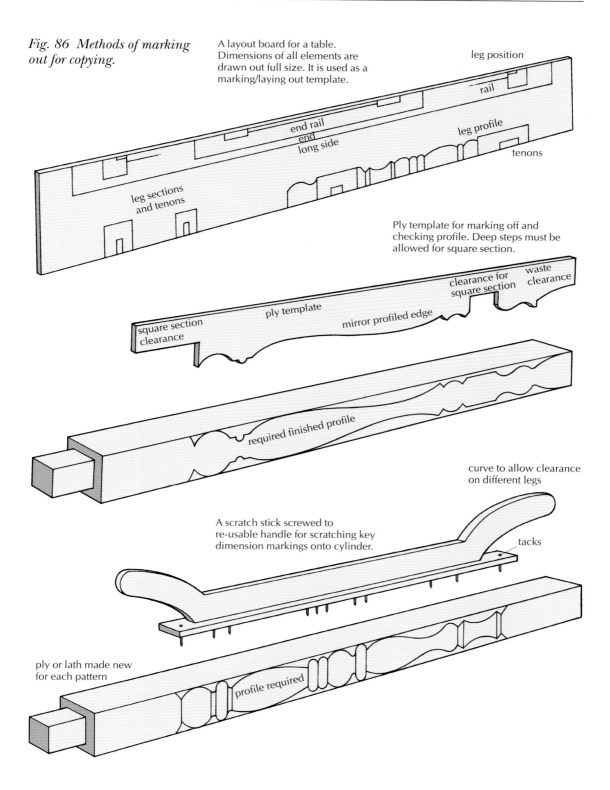

leg position

rail

end rail
end
long side

leg profile

tenons

leg sections
and tenons

Ply template for marking off and checking profile. Deep steps must be allowed for square section.

clearance for
square section

waste
clearance

square section
clearance

ply template

mirror profiled edge

required finished profile

curve to allow clearance
on different legs

A scratch stick screwed to re-usable handle for scratching key dimension markings onto cylinder.

tacks

ply or lath made new
for each pattern

profile required

Fig. 87 Copying. (Top left) the simple 'eyeing-up' method; checking against the pattern piece. (Top right) Marking off from the pattern piece. (Left) Measuring off with callipers.

right through at each of the critical points of dimension. Once the blank has been roughed to a round, the strip is held against the rotating wood so that the nail points produce ring-score marks at key points.

Another version of the marker board is a strip of ply with notches cut along the edge. The notches are of a size to position the point of a pencil, and mark off key dimensions along a rotating rounded spindle.

For a run of only a few copies there are a couple of further alternatives: one is to hold the pattern spindle close to the rotating roughed blank and then mark off key points with a pencil; or again, if using a full-length tool-rest, to put a strip of masking tape along the rest and to mark off key points on the tape. These measurements are transferred to the roughed blank using a marking pencil and/or the long point of a skew chisel.

Without a true eye and a lot of skill, however, although the 'eyeball' method will probably position the beginning and end of each feature at about the right place along the length of the spindle, it is very likely to leave you with features of varying diameters and wandering profiles. The measured-off approach is therefore more reliable for those with only moderate skill.

THE MEASURING-OFF METHOD

In this method, once the blank has been roughed to a round, the exact location of the beginning and end of each feature is scribed onto the spindle. You may still use the nail-point strip-scriber, or the marked run of masking tape, or equally you might carefully measure off each point from the pattern spindle and then use a ruler or tape to transfer the position to the blank. The scribe may then be a pencil or a skew-point-cut ring.

Some less skilled turners also find it useful to have a cardboard test template to ensure the accuracy of the profiles. However, whole length templates are difficult to offer up where only part of the spindle has been shaped, and they are particularly awkward where there are any square to round ends. Some turners therefore have a series of templates of various common standard sizes for each of the features that they cut frequently; these may not help fix the position of elements, but they do ensure more accurate profiling.

The main problems with all measured-off approaches is the time that they take, with the constant stopping and starting as each measurement is made and

transferred. Even worse is the fact that the whole process has to be repeated with each spindle. As the saying goes, there must be a better way!

There is: it is the 'copy fingers' approach. This is based upon packets of articulated 'fingers' that can be bought from Craft Supplies Ltd.

COPY FINGERS

The fingers have to be mounted on a shaft or dowel which is positioned behind (on the far side of) the spindle being turned, and just a little above the axis height. For my Poolewood 28/40 I have made a frame which clamps to the bed bars. The finger shaft is mounted on this and the whole frame can be adjusted so that the shaft can be raised or lowered, or moved in or out to accommodate different sizes of spindle, from small candlesticks to large diameter refectory table legs.

The pattern piece is turned first, and once it is finished, the dozen or so fingers are positioned along the shaft and adjusted

Fig. 88 The copy fingers are set to fall when maximum required diameters are achieved at key points.

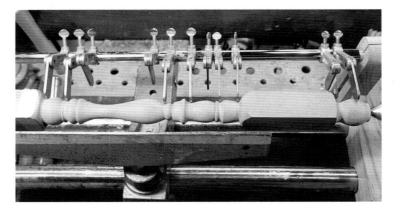

Fig. 89 The spindle is finished but some of the copy fingers have been reset to show their location on key features.

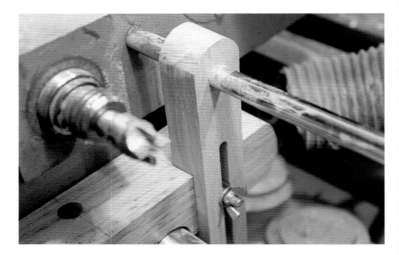

Fig. 90 The DIY mounting frame using oak and a chromed curtain rail from the ironmongers.

mum and minimum depth. The pattern piece is now taken off the mountings and is laid on the lathe bed just behind the working zone and in direct view. This can be eyed up to check the developing profiles of elements as they are cut.

Once the new blank is clamped up on the lathe, all the fingers are allowed to sit on the top of the spindle; and there they stay until the feature is worked and the finger falls through, indicating that the required (position and) dimension has been achieved. They are, in fact, sizing just as would a set of multiple external callipers.

The use of copy fingers means that after the first piece has been turned, there is no further measuring to be done and no other blank has to be marked off; once the second blank has been mounted on the lathe it can be turned without having to stop the machine at all. Starting at the outboard end each detail is worked in turn to the finished profile. The finger drop ensures the correct dimension and the location of the feature, and the eye view of the pattern ensures that the curves and profile of the copy is true to the original.

This device has reduced the time that it takes me to produce a set of four matching legs by over two-thirds, and until I reach the skill level of the great time-served spindle turners who can do everything by eye, I consider it to be the best turning-tool purchase that I have ever made.

so that the tips of the articulated ends just clear the spindle profile. In fact they are first positioned so that the tip just rests on the top of the spindle, and they are then drawn back until they just fall through the gap. At this setting they are clamped off to the shaft with their finger screws.

A finger is positioned at the beginning and end of each feature, and at key points of particular features – ie points of maxi-

— 11 —

SOME DESIGN CONSIDERATIONS

To many, the turning of between-centre items falls into the category of 'necessary evils'. Often they are things that have to be made because we need them as a part of something else. Early in our turning lives we make our own tool handles; we need a set of legs for a table; someone has asked us for a set of banister spindles: rarely are the spindles we make complete pieces in their own right, and even the simplest have face-plate-turned bases. Yet they can provide the major element in many bread-and-butter items – things that will sell at craft fairs, church fund-raising events, or local tourist gift shops: bud vases, wooden pens, finger tops, collector's eggs, candlesticks, wine tables, garden dibbers and so on. Then there are the specific commissions: a croquet set, skittle pins and other games equipment.

We do have our moments: for instance, a birthday present candlestick for a family member gives our imagination more rein. Then maybe we move into fine, elegant and challenging goblets and other more skilful areas of between-centres work.

THE FUNCTION OF SPINDLES

Spindle turners tend to be looked down upon as second-class citizens in today's world of 'art turning', and the spindle-turned piece which is sculptural, or purely decorative is a great rarity. Some seem to think that if you don't 'do' art pieces, or have work in up-market art galleries, you are not a real turner. Of course, there is some envy of us, too: some spindle turners actually make a reasonable living without having to support their turning by teaching, demonstrating or writing. Maybe there is some justification in the lack of respect – so much of the between-centres work is pedestrian or of poor design. But then, not as poor as are most of the face-plate-turned items offered for sale at most craft fairs.

It is probably a combination of facets that prompts this lack of esteem. There is no escape from the fact that the bulk of spindles are fundamentally functional, necessary evils, and usually have to be made to very keen commercial rates; it may be for this reason that so little thought appears to be given to design considerations. Even so, I am sure that if you talked about legs to Chippendale, Hepplewhite or any of the other great furniture designers and makers, you would be given a very long, studied lecture about their importance in both structural and *decorative* terms. Some of their arguments would proceed along the following lines.

'Spindles' usually form just a component part or parts of a bigger item; in many cases they are going to be built into a piece of furniture or into an internal or external architectural feature. They are hence a fundamental element in what must be a 'whole' design, and this has enormous implications. We can address this issue on five fronts: by defining the five fundamental functions of spindles, as supporting; spacing; framing; structural; and pure decoration.

SPINDLES FOR SUPPORT

Supporting spindles clearly support, but they do it in two ways. They support physically the platform and the weight that is put upon it; but they also support, in a decorative sense, the element that provides the main function of the piece. Thus chair legs support the seat and the back; table legs the table top; standard-lamp columns the light and the shade; candlesticks the candle; lectern columns the headframe and the book that will be placed upon it; music stands the headframe and the music that will be placed on that. Each of these items (and the many more that are similar) must have the structural integrity for the load they will bear; but they must also have the design integrity needed to fit in with the whole piece and its function, both real and psychological.

So there are important considerations regarding the apparently simple word 'function'. A music stand, for instance, does not just support a few sheets of music – it also has to complement the person who is using it. A conductor's stand is big, solid, and 'important' – certainly it does carry a little more weight (the whole score) than does that of a player in the orchestra, and it is also more likely to get caught by flailing arms and therefore needs to be more stable – but the stand and the music are where the work is coming from, and are the status symbol of the leader, in this case the conductor. The stand used by a soloist at a recital must also have 'presence' and complement and integrate with the performer.

In the case of lecterns there is an additional factor, because not only are most church bibles heavy and therefore in need of strong support, but they are massive and need to integrate with a substantial piece of church furniture – what is more, they clearly support the texts upon which faith is based. The additional element can be, unfortunately, that many lecterns were

Fig. 91 Victorian platform rocking chair, constructed mainly from spindle-turned elements.

donated, and their size and magnificence has the extra function of proclaiming the status and importance of the benefactor (to both God *and* the congregation!).

So the 'function' is often multi-layered. An essential question that you should always ask when considering a commission is, 'Where will it stand, and what will it be used for?' But the question should be addressed not only to locational and factual issues but to environmental and psychological matters.

SPINDLES AS SPACERS

The spacing function of spindles emerges in many examples. In most cases their task could be equally well performed by solid sheet or planking – except of course, that that would consume much more timber and probably therefore be more expensive; and it would often be 'heavy' and enclosing, where the impression that we are after is of space and lightness. The most widely encountered example is banister spindles which provide a spacing and safety barrier function between the banister rail and the body of the stairway carcass. Then there are spacers or stretchers between the legs of most chairs; and spacers within the framework of bed-heads and foot-boards.

SPINDLES IN FRAMES

There are many blurrings between the functions of spacing and framing, and even the structural role of spindles. There are picture frames made of turned elements, and many period tapestry frames and fire-screens where the outer square or rectangle frames the whole. Of course it could be argued that the frame is merely the structure to support the tapestry. So do these classifications get us anywhere? The answer must be 'Yes!'. We all like a frame which surrounds something of beauty to be beautiful itself: it must complement, raise, and set apart that which it frames, though without swamping or distracting from the contents. There are even more important implications that will emerge when we consider the 'eye flow'.

THE STRUCTURAL CAPACITY OF SPINDLES

The structural element function of a spindle is different from its structural integrity. Integrity is concerned with the strength of the *material*, and with using sufficient material of an appropriate nature and diameter, such that the spindles will stand up to the use (or function) to which they will be employed. Thus the handle is an essential structural element of the tool. The various components (with the possible exception of the supporting legs) of a spinning wheel are structural elements: they could be made of any material, not only wood, and in functional terms the decoration is purely coincidental; they are all there to fulfil sub-functions of the spinning process. Shafts, spindles, handles, threaded tensioners, dowels and pegs can all be considered as structural elements. Of course, table and chair legs are also structural elements, but as we have already seen, their size, shape and decoration all have important and quite specific secondary functions.

THE DECORATIVE FUNCTION

Since time began, Man has decorated the things that he has made, and the more important or special the item, the more loving care is spent on decoration. Few examples can epitomize this better than can the spinning wheel, and even the earliest, crude models had decoration incised into them. A man made one for his wife, girlfriend or child, and demonstrated his love for that person by investing in it his greatest skills and craftsmanship and by the care he took and the decoration he worked into the design. So in this sense it might be argued that even their decoration has a 'function' – as an expression of love!

Later, decoration became a means of demonstrating quality, superiority of craftsmanship and concern for design in the items made for sale. It gave market standing to the producer (and a justification for charging premium-plus prices!). It has also been identified as having no other function than to be decorative, thus distinguishing one small category of spindles from all the many which, while decorated, and sometimes extensively – are primarily there for one of the other four functions. So here we are concerned with spindles, often split turnings, that are integrated into a piece of furniture for purely decorative purposes;

the split-turned pieces that are often placed on each side of the face of long-case and other clocks are typical examples.

THE VISUAL INFLUENCE OF DECORATION

The significance of this five function separation becomes apparent when we look at the question of eye appeal, and particularly of eye flow or travel, and what this means in terms of the design of the decoration. In considering the design of a spindle we have to be conscious of where it fits within the whole and where we want to direct the eye. First, the whole has to be satisfying and integrated: you don't want anything to stand out awkwardly and to specifically hold the eye; you want to sweep the eye towards the focal point of the whole piece.

In the Standard Lamp
For instance, you want the viewer to take in the whole balance and proportion of the standard lamp, and we have to recognize that the lamp will probably stand near an important easy chair or settee. Clearly, and probably primarily, the lamp has to be both truly and obviously stable, and this will mean a base of suitable weight and footprint. By keeping the 'heavy' base relatively simple, the eye will quickly become satisfied with the stability it presents, and will be ready to move on. Alternatively the base could be of tripod leg form, as this naturally 'pushes' the eye upwards. An important role of a standard lamp is to provide a point of interest which is higher than that of most of the other pieces of furniture – they really do provide 'high points' in the overall shape of the room.

Ultimately you want the eye to be carried up to the lamp and the shade, and you do this by tapering the column up from the base, and by the selection and placing of the decorative features; in this way you give the eye an easy passage. The features near the

Fig. 92 A candelabrum made from three spigot-jointed sections. The base was glue-block turned, and the bun feet on a screw chuck. The front legs of the Prie chairs were between-centres turned in Padauk.

base are therefore, larger, widely spaced and longer, because this gives the clear impression that the lamp grows up out of the floor rather than hanging down from the ceiling: a standard lamp gives emphasis to the height of the room while the suspended lamp brings down the ceiling. Also the features we turn on the column can push the passage of the eye upwards. Ogees have a sharply rounded end and a long taper, so the round end should be placed at the bottom whilst the gentle slope of the taper carries the eye 'freewheeling' easily on to the next feature or short-stay point of interest.

In short, the travel of the eye must be assisted, that is, pushed along in the required direction; and it must be comfortable.

Spindles to Add Interest

The eye glides along a narrowing taper because the natural movement is from a larger diameter to a smaller. We tend to look at the *peaks* of mountains, pausing only briefly to assimilate their bases and slopes. A particular crag may arrest the eye for a moment, just as an interrupting bead adds a little interest in our journey up the lamp column and prevents the journey from being too boring. But overdo the beads, and the journey becomes bumpy and uncomfortable. A big vertical facing cut – or worse, a beak or bell-shaped overhang has to be 'surmounted' by the eye; and this requires real effort, just as this sort of feature would to a climber on the cliff face. A series of button beads with a cove between each is as tiring to traverse as an alpine range (and far less interesting!)

We add punctuation marks between main features, and so include smaller beads and grooves, coves, quirks and fillets – but we have to exercise caution, because by overdoing the narrowing taper between two larger diameter ends we create tension. It looks like something being stretched apart, and if thin enough, to be near breaking. Circumferential grooves or rings cause the eye to pause and can add interest; spirals do much the same, but continue to push the eye along in a required direction. Longitudinal grooves or flutes also speed the passage of the eye.

By varying the small features we add interest but we do need some longer sweeping features to prevent the design from being too fussy. The old button bead, or bobbin reel spindles were not the most visually pleasing; a long run of identical round beads is something that most people find either dull and repetitive, or exceedingly agitating.

Spindles in Frames

Spindle-turned frames clearly present a problem. You don't want the eye to travel along them, but once it has taken in the overall decorative aspects you want it to look elsewhere, namely back at the picture, or the embroidery, or whatever it is framing. This is done by first making each opposite pair of spindles symmetrical about their centre point. Ideally all four sides should be of the same profile although possibly scaled slightly to different lengths. The eye comes to rest at the centre of a symmetrical pattern, so if all four are similar it is pushed into the centre of the whole frame.

... in Bowls and Banisters

We often see the same convention used in producing the spindles supporting the rail in galleried bowls. With all of these it is usual to find that the design is symmetrical on both sides of the centre. Most frequently, too, the diameter is greater at the centre than at the ends. On the other hand there is no clear convention for banister spindles; where there are two schools of thought: one is the symmetrical group, while the other favours the 'sweep the eye upwards' approach. Clearly no one sees the banister rail as needing rugged structural support, or as floating above the stairs.

THE DECORATIVE REQUIREMENT IN LEGS

So legs have the basic function of supporting; but if that was all we wanted, we would just use old tea-chests. Much more important is the decorative requirement – not just the pure visual impact of the shapes, but more in the effects we want to cause in the eye and thus create in the brain.

At a woodturning seminar a dedicated 'bowlie' was holding forth and decrying the skills of the spindle turner: 'Turning legs is dull!' he said. 'Legs only support things – they are uninteresting'. At that moment a very attractive young lady turner walked by and his eager eyes appreciatively weighed up the 'mere supports' between hemline and shoes!

THE PSYCHOLOGICAL ELEMENT IN DESIGN

A leg is not just a support. In both design (profile) and decoration it must meet structural, psychological and aesthetic requirements. Not only must it *be* strong enough for the loads and forces it is to bear; it must also *look* strong enough. There are people who are very uncomfortable crossing bridges suspended on ultra-strong, but very thin section, high tensile, steel suspension wires; yet they feel quite safe on old stone bridges that may look rugged, but that are barely strong enough to support a well laden packhorse. We all know which one will get swept away in a flood!

There is a further psychological element in an item's apparent strength. We think of a table as being laden with food, and of it therefore being imperative that it has legs capable of supporting the perceived weight. Yet we sit 'comfortably' at that table – all 12 to 15 stone (76 to 95kg) of us – on chairs with legs of only a half of the diameter of those of the table itself. In fact, in normal use each chair is probably carrying five times the weight of everything on the table!

Apparent stability is another important psychological factor affecting overall design. Bowl turners will already be familiar with the concept of 'growing from' and 'floating above' design features. By lowering the apparent centre of gravity, and particularly by having bases of larger diameters than the top, we create forms that appear to have their roots in the ground; nothing could appear more stable. Alternatively, by making the top bigger and the base smaller, thus raising the centre of gravity, we can reach a stage where the object appears to float above the floor or table upon which it is placed.

We therefore need to think very carefully about the design of a piece of furniture, and whether we want it to be 'stable' and 'grow from', or be light, elegant, even ephemeral, and 'float above'. Tapered legs on chairs makes them 'float above', and lifts the person sitting on them off the floor and 'up to the table' (actually we sit down!). The legs are heavier at the top than they are at the foot because it is at the head that we require both actual and apparent strength.

TABLES

The fine legs, or the deep hidden single central pedestal of Regency tables, made them 'float'; this was very appropriate to the frothy elegance of Regency times. A big meal was achieved through many successive courses of reasonable proportions. The earlier simple refectory table on the other hand may have seen the frugality of a more austere monastery; but in its normal decorated domestic form it is associated with the manor hall and massive meals where much of the food was presented at the same time. The table needed to be solid and to appear to grow out of the earth!

FOUR-POSTER BEDS

We can see a similar interplay between the practical, structural, psychological and aesthetic when we look at four-poster beds, and particularly at how they have changed over the centuries. In medieval times those who could afford the privilege of not sleeping on the floor together with a large number of others (their family, servants, soldiers and so on), built large cupboard-like constructions into the walls of the room. These afforded privacy, intimacy, warmth and above all, some draught-proofing.

As rooms became bigger and the bed moved out from being a wall cupboard, beds retained their box-like structure of draught-proofing – in fact they were still timber-framed 'houses'. There was a solid headboard and the planked canopy, but now the sides consisted of heavy drapes. Full height legs were still required to support the outboard end of the canopy, and these continued to be 'over engineered' 'frame members'. However, in order to make the bed something special, they were then heavily ornamented with intricate carving.

Later designs moved away from the massive Jacobean and Tudor oak structures. Even many of the less wealthy houses began to have glass in the window apertures, and were generally just a little more draught free. Where the owner still wanted a four-poster, it gradually developed to be a light, frothy affair with fine curtains and a woven canopy. The legs could be lighter, so shape and diameter moved towards the fine elegance that became most refined in the Regency designs. The four-poster became a frilly love nest, a connotation that it has preserved to this day.

THE STRESS FORCES ON CHAIRS AND TABLES

Moving from the psychological to the real structural function, and looking again at the chair, we have already identified that its legs need to be many times stronger than do those of the table. We can also see why legs can, and frequently do taper from top to bottom. Of course a taper gives the piece grace and elegance; but there is more to it than that.

On both chair and table there is a vertical weight-bearing function. In fact, on both, this compression strength could be achieved with quite thin sections of any reasonable, straight grained wood. Unfortunately we often move tables by lifting one end and dragging the other two feet across the carpet: in doing this we are applying a bending moment to the leg, and an enormous 'pulling apart' moment on the top joint.

With chairs it is even worse: we drag them in closer to the table without fully taking our weight right off; we lean against the

back; in the expansiveness of our cups we may even tilt back on the rear legs; of course we climb on them to get to the top shelf of the cupboard; we put heavy boxes on them while rummaging through the contents; and so on. The loadings we put on the legs and all four seat joints can be colossal, and the greatest concentration of forces is around the top of the legs. Hence we make legs more robust at the top, and then taper them down to the much more lightly-loaded and stressed foot.

There are exceptions to the generality of tapering legs: one is the four-legged refectory-type table. Here the legs are very close to the corners of the table top, they go straight down, and are tied around the base by a foot-rail along all four sides. Like this the legs and cross-members form the frame of a box – a high-strength structure which resists dragging and twisting forces. We also 'expect' a frame to be of square, straight timber. You do not want the table top to be 'floating' (as on fine, tapered legs), but to be sitting firmly, four square, on the floor.

DECORATION MUST BE RELATIVE

This concept has a strong bearing upon all the decoration we apply, in that it has to be in keeping with the element it is carved into, and with the whole psychological function of the piece. Moreover, there are other, purely aesthetic considerations that have led to generally accepted design conventions. The first is that the proportions of each element should conform to classic design principles; thus a good ogee looks very much better if it uses the golden rule of classic thirds proportions.

Overall there is a notional 'ratio' between the diameter and the length of both frame and in-fill elements: the longer the piece, the greater will be its diameter. Often the

Fig. 93 A disc-bead-turned bed. The rounded shoulders were turned as a large ring which was then cut into four quadrants.

difference will be only a millimetre or two, and certainly not sufficient to give any significant difference in bending strength.

It is also both an aesthetic and a practical norm for the square end sections of a turned leg to be of larger cross-section than are any of the turned parts. It is clearly useful to have square sections where side members abut vertical frame elements, because it is much easier to make accurately angled, precisely dimensioned mortises and tenon joins into and onto the face of squared-section timber. Accurately drilling a mortise into a round section is not easy, particularly where a correct angle (sometimes off-set) has to be achieved between two adjacent mortises.

So frequently we get legs with a squared section at each end to facilitate frame-jointing, and the two squared sections then act as a frame to 'contain' the decoration between.

Historically, turners made a lot of furniture; and most good furniture makers were highly skilled on the lathe. It was bowl turning that was at the bottom end of the market and of the ability range. Back in the sixteenth century quality chairs took one of two forms: they were either made totally of plank construction, and the best were then decorated with carving; or they were constructed almost entirely of turned elements. A range of chairs popular at about this time were known as 'thrown chairs' because the whole frame consisted of intricately turned elements or 'spindles'.

In England, furniture legs slowly developed to being cleaner in design, a little less massive in construction, and much easier to turn. In France, turned furniture also became more sophisticated, and button-turned pieces appeared. Some of their button-turned bed-head and foot-frames demonstrate a truly remarkable level of skill.

Of course decoration is addictive to the turner, but like all drugs it can be abused: if over-done, both bring death! Working in a lot of different and difficult features may well demonstrate how clever you are with tools, but it also shows that you are far from clever with design. It can certainly kill with fussiness what might otherwise be a nice piece of furniture.

THE DECORATIVE PROPENSITIES OF DIFFERENT WOODS

Finally, we need to come back to an issue touched upon earlier. There is an important interaction between the variety of wood used and the decoration that is applied to it. Some woods will cut easily and into fine detail; others by their very nature tend to tolerate only simple carving and therefore only broad decoration. Fine, very straight-grained woods will support, and even call for more complex design – more interesting features, more frequent and more closely spaced. Woods with wild grain (and elm in a supreme example) will not carve easily into fine decoration and is much more likely to chip on a projecting feature.

Darker woods do not really 'carry' fine decoration; and very light woods often look best if not decorated at all. Think of the beautiful simplicity of undecorated, clean-

Fig. 94 A button-bead turned corner chair: it is not a very inspiring design, probably a turner's 'show-off' piece.

line, Scandinavian white ash-based furniture. Of course many generally accepted conventions are historically rooted in very practical issues. Oak, for a long time the most widely used furniture and building material in all but the cheapest ends of the market, is hard to work. It can be carved to a reasonable level of detail, but it takes time. Can you imagine producing a fine, reed-fluted oak leg with a scratch stock – for this is what was mainly used on mahogany legs until the router came along.

BREAKING THE RULES

A lot of what we have been exploring in this chapter are not so much rules or 'conventions' but more the underlying reasons behind so many of the established norms.

As a lecturer said to me at art school many years ago: 'You can always break the rules –

if you do it deliberately and clearly you can often achieve an interesting required effect. It can shock and stimulate the interest of the viewer. Do it unconsciously, and all the time and you create confusion and rejection.' He was an Impressionist and abstract painter and occasionally he would place two warring colours side by side; put in some small detail that you could not understand and had to think about; or draw a line so thin that you expected it to snap. The effect was always powerful and dramatic because it created a feeling of tension – but it was made the more so by the fact that the entire rest of the work conformed to all the rules of proportion, balance, and colour toning and placing that you would find in the traditional old masters. He sold all he ever painted, and was hung in both the most respected and the most *avant garde* galleries.

In the drawings overleaf there are a number of designs for legs of various types for different pieces of furniture. Most were taken from, or were based upon traditional designs. The dimensions have been given, but these must only be used as a guide to ratios. You may wish to increase or decrease the length by an inch or so (2–3cm) (to alter the height of the table). The diameters may be altered a millimetre or two, or elements from different designs may be combined. The materials you are working with will affect the choice of the design and the dimensions. Oak furniture tends towards simpler shapes and often to slightly heavier proportions; mahogany to the light and detailed.

CONCLUSION

Let us now summarize a few of the principles that we have been developing.

1. Any single shape or element should itself be based upon classic principles of proportion.
2. Shapes that are placed together should

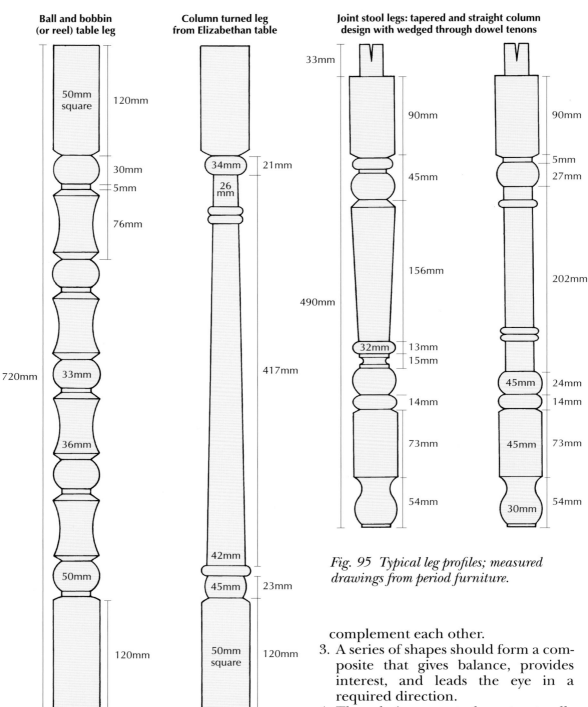

Ball and bobbin (or reel) table leg

50mm square — 120mm
30mm
5mm
76mm
33mm
36mm
50mm
720mm
120mm

Column turned leg from Elizabethan table

34mm — 21mm
26mm
417mm
42mm
45mm — 23mm
50mm square — 120mm

Joint stool legs: tapered and straight column design with wedged through dowel tenons

33mm
90mm
45mm
156mm
490mm
32mm — 13mm
15mm
14mm
73mm
54mm

90mm
5mm
27mm
202mm
45mm — 24mm
14mm
45mm — 73mm
54mm
30mm

Fig. 95 Typical leg profiles; measured drawings from period furniture.

complement each other.
3. A series of shapes should form a composite that gives balance, provides interest, and leads the eye in a required direction.
4. The design must be structurally sound.
5. The elements must not only *be* structurally sound, but they must *look* sound.
6. Tension or shock is rarely appropriate in

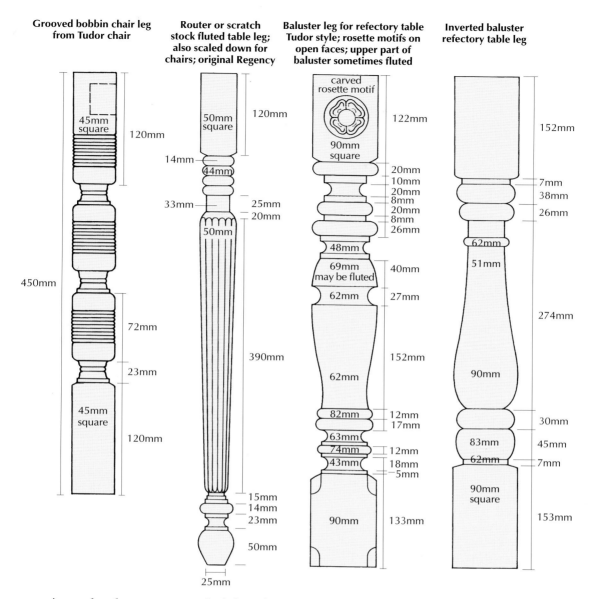

Grooved bobbin chair leg from Tudor chair

Router or scratch stock fluted table leg; also scaled down for chairs; original Regency

Baluster leg for refectory table Tudor style; rosette motifs on open faces; upper part of baluster sometimes fluted

Inverted baluster refectory table leg

carved rosette motif

pieces that have any practical function.

7. Where the item is an element of something larger, it should not be fussy, excessively decorated or detailed, and it should certainly *not* be distracting.
8. The elements add most to the quality of the whole by their precision and crispness of detail.
9. The more the element is an item in its own right, the more appropriate are innovation and clever design features.
10. The essence of spindle-turning design is delicacy and precision, and there is little place for the ruggedness and country-style work that can be effective in bowl turning.
11. Spindles are not appropriate vehicles for displaying the startling nature of highly figured woods.
12. The fundamental purpose of any and every spindle is to be functional, given that even 'decoration' can be a function. The design of the item and the whole must always be true to that function.

12

SPIRALS AND BARLEY TWIST

At one time a lot of the decoration on spindles was hand-carved; indeed the massive legs on Tudor and Jacobean four-poster beds were rarely turned, and even the rounded sections were hand-worked. This is hardly surprising; however, just imagine turning a 6ft (1.8m) length of 5in (13cm) square-section oak on a pole lathe! Even today we see some hand-carving on spindles: a Tudor rose on the square section at the top of a reproduction refectory table leg; the fluting on a table leg; the mouse on the leg of every piece of furniture made by Thomsons of Kilburn.

When the idea of twist decoration – particularly the ever-popular barley twist – first came in, this was again seen as a problem to which hand-working was the answer. Today we have the option of hand or machine; but the machine used is not the conventional lathe and the forming is done with power routers. Lathes will not turn slowly enough to allow even a skilled carver with really sharp tools to cut controlled spiral grooves. You would probably need a turning speed of less than one revolution every five minutes or so. You would also need great skill to co-ordinate the sideways sweep of the tool with the turning of the cylinder, to get an even spiral.

Some of the advanced copy lathes do provide the necessary facilities where the travel of the cutting head is precisely synchronized with the speed of rotation of the spindle. But as has already been stressed such machines need a huge capital investment.

A number of innovative turners have produced devices of their own which couple the rotation of the spindle to the sideways travel of a router carriage; and articles describing their experiments have appeared on a number of occasions in *Woodworker* and other magazines.

Trend, ever known for exploring additional ways of exploiting the potential of the router, now offer a hobbyist-level unit along the same lines, and we will be examining this in detail later.

There are turners who still carve spirals by hand; indeed, two of the best insist that they can carve a barley twist on a table leg as fast by hand as they can by special machine when the time taken to set up the machine is taken into account. So let's look at the hand cutting of spirals and twists; but first we will explain the names and technical terms of aspects of twists.

THE THREE FORMS OF TWIST

There are three forms of twist to consider.

BARLEY TWIST

The traditional barley twist is where there are one, two or three 'Bines' or strands each of which makes one revolution every 2 or 3in (5 or 7½cm) (known as a 'Lead' of 2 or 3in). One convention with a 'Double Bine' twist is that it makes one complete revolution over a length which equates with the diameter of the spindle; hence a 2in (5cm) diameter leg would have a bine going right round once over a 2in length. You do, however, see many patterns and sizes, and the most frequent is

Fig. 96 A beautiful Norwegian spinning wheel. Wheels are probably the ultimate example of the spindle turner's art.

with the bine's revolution spread along a distance of one-and-a-half and even two times the spindle's diameter. Certainly increasing the number of bines requires a lengthening of the pitch. Many reproduction gate-leg tables and dinner wagons with barley-twist legs are double bine with a two times lead-to-diameter ratio.

PIERCED TWIST

The second form of twist – much more difficult to execute and therefore less frequently seen – is the pierced twist, where each bine of the rope is separated from the others and 'you can see daylight through the middle'. Two-bine twists are encountered, but three

and four are preferred as they provide considerably greater strength. A competent barley-twist carver will find no difficulty in producing pierced twists.

ROPE TWIST

The third form of spiralling sometimes seen is known as a 'rope twist'; it is in effect a spiral fluting or reeding. The difficulty here is that while minor deviations and variations in the carving are not noticed on the broad ropes of a barley twist, they are blindingly obvious on the much smaller and precise reeds. Before tackling spiral-rope reed cutting by hand, the turner needs to spend a lot of time developing carving skills. This form of twist is, however, very easy to produce on the Trend Routerlathe and similar devices.

HAND-CUTTING BARLEY TWISTS

This is a relatively simple process and is best done with the spindle mounted on the lathe. You can hand-rotate the blank as you work along it and it is at a good height for carving. This process is made much easier if the lathe is fitted with a full index head, which helps considerably during marking out, and will lock the spindle in set positions during carving.

The most difficult part of producing twists is the setting out, and then working to the setting-out marks made! Until you cut spirals regularly and develop an eye for layout, it is advisable to pre-test alternative pitch lengths or spacings. This is done with a length of string or long strips of paper.

PREPARING THE SPINDLE

First, turn the spindle to the basic form and profile that you require. Ideally you should design it such that the length to be twist-

Fig. 97 A triumph of fluted spindles!

carved is a multiple of the diameter. Cut the square-to-round shoulders, and any other detail – feet and suchlike – and then plane down to a cylinder the length that is to be carved. If you intend to have a small cove at each end of the twist – which is a common arrangement – this is better left until after carving as it helps to tidy up the ends of the flutes and bines.

SETTING OUT THE TWIST

Now take a piece of string and fix one end to the spindle with masking tape at a point where the bine will start. If you are cutting a one-bine twist, decide where you want the twist to start in relation to any square section, and whether you want the twists on all legs to start in the same position. You now wind the string along the spindle to simulate the lie of the rope of the twist. Try various levels of lapping until you get a proportion that appeals to you. Try out a 1:1 lap-to-diameter ratio, then 1:1½ and so on. Finally, measure the wave-top to wave-top distance (the lead) for a complete revolution on one rope; this will give you the pitch you are going to work – the 'pitch' being the distance between adjacent bine crests (hence it is the lead dis-tance divided by the number of bines in the twist).

You may wish to develop this idea for testing possible layouts. For instance, using two or three different coloured pieces of string, you can test out the lie of all the ropes in a multi-bine spiral.

It is much easier to work to whole, round number measurements, so unless you are a mathematician, you will probably find it better to round up or down on the measured pitch distance and relate this to the total length of the carved section.

MARKING UP THE SPINDLE

You now need to mark lines along the length of the spindle from the start point of each bine, and this procedure is much easier if you have an index head. If you do not have an indexer and you are working on a spindle with no squared section, then, using a protractor, carefully mark on the end of the spindle the start point for each of the bines that you require. Two bines start diagonally opposite each other on the spindle end; three bines are at 120 degrees to each other; and four bines on opposite quadrants. Carry the marks over the edge onto the spindle face. With a square-ended spindle, measure off and mark the required bine start-points on the faces of the square, starting either at a corner or a mid-face – the choice is yours.

Set the tool-rest at exactly the height of the lathe's axis. This can be done by removing the spindle and aligning the top of the rest with the head- and tailstock points. Now hand-rotate the spindle until the first of the bine end marks aligns with the top of the tool rest, and with a pencil on the top of the rest draw a line along the section to be carved. Do this for each of the bines.

With a 48-hole index head you do not need to mark off the end of the spindle, but simply position the indexer so that hole 0/48 coincides with the required start of the first bine. Clamp the indexer ring in this position. Now select holes 0/48 and 24 for double bine; 0/48, 16 and 32 for three-bine; and 0/48, 12, 24 and 36 for four-bine twists. Again, mark off a corresponding number of horizontal lines.

For the moment we will consider only a double-bine twist. For this you will have two diagonally opposite lines down the spindle. The main one we will call the datum line, the other the second line.

MARKING RINGS ON THE SPINDLE

The next task is to mark rings on the spindle to correspond with the lead distance of one twist. Scale these off with a ruler, hold the pencil on the mark and hand-rotate the spindle to provide a circular mark. Number or letter the points where the rings intersect the datum line. Let us call them A, B, C, D, E and so on.

Rotate the cylinder through 180 degrees until you are looking at the second line. Make marks along this line exactly half-way between each pair of the previously draw adjacent rings (preferably using a different colour of pencil). Number these 1, 2, 3, 4, etc.

Fig. 98 (Top) Drawing out a barley twist.
(Bottom) Cutting sequence for barley twists.

DRAWING THE SPIRALS

You now have to draw the spiral which represents the crest of the first complete bine. This means joining point A on to 1, then on round to B and on to 2, and round to C, and so on. For the first few carvings some 'twisters' wrap a narrow strip of masking tape round to mark the line of the spiral.

Before marking off the spiral for the second bine, it is advisable to make a saw cut which marks the bottom of the trough between each spiral of the first bine. This is done with a tenon saw held vertically but angled to parallel the rope peaks and exactly half-way between them. The depth of the cut is a little less than the finished depth of the trough.

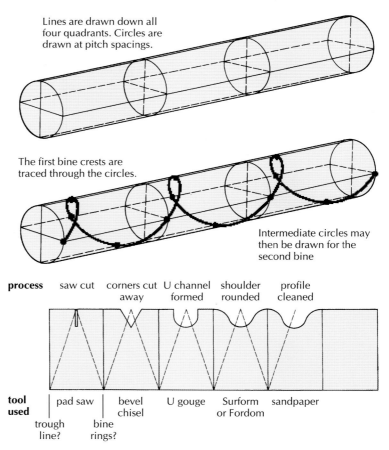

Lines are drawn down all four quadrants. Circles are drawn at pitch spacings.

The first bine crests are traced through the circles.

Intermediate circles may then be drawn for the second bine

process	saw cut	corners cut away	U channel formed	shoulder rounded	profile cleaned
tool used	pad saw	bevel chisel	U gouge	Surform or Fordom	sandpaper
	trough line?	bine rings?			

For safety it is wise to put a stop mark on the blade of the tenon saw: this is a run of masking tape which shows the depth to cut to.

Now rotate the spindle until the second straight line is before you, and where this intersects with the ring marks, you will have the line for the apex of the second bine. Complete the drawing of this spiral. Now locate the trough for this bine and again, saw groove this.

Using a sharp bevel chisel, the tenon saw cuts are now widened to vee-form troughs. These may be cleaned out using a Veiner carving tool, although it is not essential to do so.

CARVING AND SANDING

The main carving task is to open out the vee grooves with a gouge to form first of all the deeper zone of a clean trough. The shoulders are then cut away and rounded over, first with a flat chisel and then using a rasp or Surform tool.

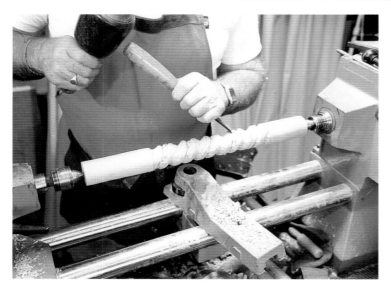

Fig. 99 (Top) The coloured lines marking the troughs are cut with a pad saw to the full depth required.
(Above) The shoulders are cut away with a ½in bevel chisel. Here the second trough is just being started.
(Left) Still using the bevel chisel, rounding over has started.

(Left) A shallow U-gouge rounds out the depth of the groove.

(Below) A round Surform file finishes the basic shaping.

(Below) A power burr or sander is useful for shaping and finishing. Here a Fordom is being used, but a Minicraft or a Dremmel would be quite satisfactory.

(Right) The final finishing has to be with hand held-abrasives. A length of rubber hose is less wearing than an index finger! 180, 320 and then 400 grit papers are used.

The surface is cleaned with a newly sharpened gouge and chisel, and is sanded smooth, first coarse sanding, with the abrasive paper wrapped around a short section of garden hose, then fine sanding. This still uses the hose length as a sanding block, but it has to be done with the lathe at rest to ensure that you get down into the troughs.

There are two alternative sanding methods. One uses strips of sanding cloth, but probably the best and the simplest is to use small-diameter flap wheels on a drill. The advantage of the latter method is that the direction of sanding can now be very nearly along the grain, whereas with abrasive paper and cloth sanding it is along the spiral.

CUTTING MULTI-BINE TWISTS

The complications in cutting multi-bine twists start at the marking-out stage. Obviously the principles are the same, however many ropes; the difficulty is in keeping track of which bine you are working on. For this reason it is often useful to draw each bine apex as a pencil line, but then to trace out each trough with a coloured spiral, each in a different colour. Coloured marker pens are ideal for this purpose. It is here that saw-cutting the groove before you move on to draw the next spiral helps to keep you on track.

The longer the pitch and the fewer the bines, the easier it is to mark, stay on track, hand-cut, sand *and* finish!

MAKING PIERCED-THROUGH SPIRALS

Different turners/carvers adopt different approaches to making pierced-through spirals, the third of our basic forms of twist. 'Pierced-through' is where the ropes are separated, so obviously you cannot have piercing on a single rope twist, and even a two-rope twist is a little too flimsy when pierced. The norm is therefore three strands, although you do find four bines on some larger diameter pieces. It has to be said that the four-rope arrangement is rarely produced by hand-cutting methods: it is a job for the expert!

Some skilled craftsmen, having made the initial vee grooves with a tenon saw, then carry on working right through with Veiner and gouge, gradually removing the core of the piece. Others, once they have formed the basic trough as in non-pierced work, go on to drill a series of holes through the bottom of the trough and then link the drill holes, thus removing the timber from the centre gradually.

An easier approach used by some on two-bine spindles is to work up the trough lines drilling a series of holes right through the spindle before doing anything else. If they are going to make saw cuts, this is done next, and the holes are then linked. Some, however, use only drill holes and then cut between them with Veiner and gouge and even with a key-hole saw. Of course you can only drill right through a double or four-bine spindle: on a three-bine the depth of the drill holes may only exceed the radius of the spindle by the merest fraction; more than this and you will be drilling into the back of the opposite bine.

Quite nice twist decoration can be achieved using a hand-controlled router or a die grinder in a bracket such as the Techlink (*see* Chapter 14). Traditional craftsmen tend to eschew such approaches, however.

HAND-WORK VERSUS POWER TOOL

This does bring us to a question and to an area of considerable conflict. On the one side are the skilled craftsmen who regularly make carved and twist legs. By long practice they have developed the skills to do this in a traditional method, using hand tools only, and by frequent use they both maintain the skills and have developed the speed necessary to make the operation viable.

Allied to this group are those who are committed to the idea that the means are as important as the ends, and who therefore spend time on developing the necessary skills to do a reasonable job. They are the dedicated and skilled amateurs who take enormous and justified pride in their work – but who in their whole lifetime will only make a dozen or so items.

At the other end of the scale are those who do not have the time to develop a full capability in traditional skills, and who are more interested in the ends rather than the means. Their satisfaction is in a completed piece of work, even if the way that it was produced ignores some of the time-worn conventions. Even so, I know that I would rather make three pieces on which the reeding and beading looked good although it was cut with a router, than I would in only producing one piece in which all the decoration was achieved with laborious hours of scratch-stock wielding. But then perhaps this is not 'the other end

of the scale', for there is a lot of skill required to use routers and similar properly, and the true 'other end' is the fully mechanized, automatic production unit.

Fortunately, although there are still a few die-hard traditionalists who eschew any form of power tool, the margins are becoming blurred. It is not just a matter of the craft world becoming slapdash and de-skilled, but more to a genuine recognition that there are real skills in using appropriate machines and aids properly, and that to use a pillar drill and mortise bits competently requires just as much skill as it does to cut a mortise and tenon with saw, chisel and mallet. And that will, in a moment, bring us to a chapter on routerlathes as a means of producing fluted, spiral and twist spindles at a craft and hobby level.

MAKING SAWN SPIRALS

Another idea which produces very interesting, though fragile twist-style spindles is to saw them out with a tenon saw. A very skilled exponent in this field is Ian Durrant, the turner who developed the OCA off-centre chucking system (featured in a

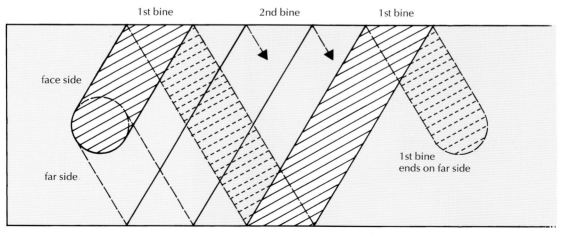

Fig. 100 Marking up for drilled spirals.

123

later chapter). Ian produces short candlesticks of a very delicate nature. A spindle blank is mounted in a collet chuck on the lathe using a glue block so that it may be held at one end only, and the cylinder is turned to a diameter which is ½–1in (13–25mm) greater than is that of the saw-tooth bit in use (such bits are, of course, available in a range of diameters).

MARKING OFF

The spindle is next marked off to a required twist, usually double bine. This time, however, both sides of the trough are defined and cut with the tenon to a slightly greater depth than the finished thickness of the bine; hence a 2in diameter saw tooth and a 2½in (6cm) diameter spindle would have saw cuts of ⅜in (9mm) depth.

When making barley twists, the tenon saw mark is cut away with gouges and accuracy is not, therefore, critical. On the twist that we are now looking at there are two parallel saw cuts which form the sides of the bine (unless the sides are to be secondarily worked); for this reason, take care to get the tenon-saw blade-angle right so that a clean, continuous cut can be made.

THE SPIRAL CUTS

The saw-tooth bit is sharpened to a keen edge and the entire core of the spindle is slowly and carefully drilled out, working from the open end only. It is not practical to try to turn the cylinder round and to remount it so that it may be drilled from the other end, because the part-worked structure would not sustain the load of drilling. This may mean using an extension drive on the bit, and the process requires great caution and patience to ensure that the bit runs true, and that no friction loading is exerted on the drilled section. The process can really only be sustained in fine-grained hardwood.

During drilling, frequent withdrawal and cooling periods are required. When re-starting after a pause, position the bit inside the mouth of the hollow before switching on the lathe. This reduces the risk of an edge catch which could ruin the piece. Before the bit is withdrawn, a puff of French chalk blown into the flutes will reduce the friction.

Finally, the ends of the spirals of wood left in the 'troughs' are cut through at a number of points, and the spiral is carefully broken out.

Fig. 101 Making a hollow spiral starts with two full-depth, pad-saw cuts. These should be parallel and have vertical walls.

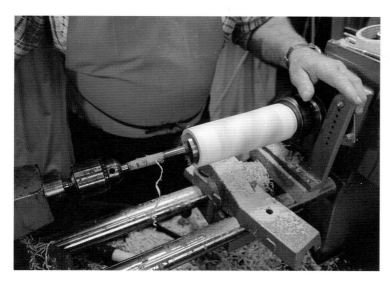

Fig. 102 The second stage involves drilling out the core. Here a saw-tooth bit is used.

FINISHING OFF

The sides of the bines now need cleaning. You have various options: leaving the edges square, rounding over, or chamfering the inside (or outside) edge. A power file and small-diameter, round sanding arbours are very useful. Careful hand-working can produce nice results, and offers scope for interesting design modifications.

(Above)
Fig. 103 The drilling is complete. The inner edges have been stained to provide contrast for the illustration. From here the edges can be cleaned to a square, or flared off.

Fig. 104 And this is what it can look like. Two examples of Ian Durrant's superb work.

13

OFF-CENTRE TURNING

Much earlier it was stated that the purpose of the lathe was to make round objects, some of which we may decorate with turned and therefore 'round' decoration. While this is fundamentally true, it is not absolute. The lathe can also be used for making things out of round – still with rounded aspects, but not truly round. Ovals are easy, and some more complex profiles and sections are not impossible. Then of course we can also turn items where the axis of the rounded elements is displaced from what is the apparent centre. It is all a matter of experimenting with moving the axis of rotation.

TURNING OUT OF ROUND

Let's start with one of the easiest arrangements. Take a 3in (7.6cm) square blank; as this is an experimental run, use a piece of inexpensive wood somewhere between 8 and 12in (20 and 30cm) long.

MARKING OUT

First find the centres by joining the diagonally opposite corners. Then along one of the diagonals mark off a second and third 'centre' off-set by ⅝in (16mm) either side of the true centre. Do the same at the outboard end so that the three centres mirror image those on the drive end and lie along the same plane. Impress all 'centres' with the drive spur.

Mount the blank on the lathe between centres, and working to the true centre,

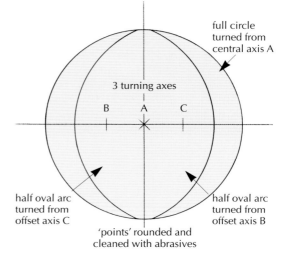

Fig. 105 Mounting axes for oval turning.

rough to a round and then plane to a burnished finish.

CUTTING

At 1in (25mm) in from each end, cut in a symmetrical cove about ¾in (20mm) wide and ½in (13mm) deep. Aim for a good off-the-tool finish, but you may clean up the trough with a little sandpaper if needed.

Now set the lathe speed down to 400–500rpm and re-mount the blank on the first pair of off-set centres. Make sure that the workpiece on the lathe is well illuminated. Pick up your medium bowl gouge.

With the spindle turning off centre there is no hard edge to the image; there are in fact a number of penumbra of differing degrees of density. If the light is strong enough you will see a shadowy image along the top edge, and towards each end you can just see where the coves are.

The advantage of the two coves will now become apparent, in that they provide a good access for the bowl gouge to start the cut. Position the gouge so that the tip is just in one of the coves and advance the tip in towards the wood until cutting contact is made. You will not be able to see the edge that you are working to at all. However, you can see the tool tip and you control the depth of cut by keeping the shavings small. Once contact is achieved start to move the gouge sideways and cut about ⅛in (3mm) deep off the spindle until you reach the cove at the other end, and cutting stops.

For the whole of this pass the tool will only be in contact for a very short time on each revolution. Obviously you watch the tool tip closely as you commence each pass, but once contact has been made and the sideways sweep has begun, watch the shadowy image on the top of the spindle. You will see a slight step indicating both the position of the gouge and the depth of cut. You control the turning process from this image!

Continue taking light passes. On each subsequent cut the contact time will increase slightly, and the top edge image will become slightly more dense. As the cut will still be intermittent, tool control is not easy. Once you have started each pass and cutting contact has been achieved, you have to move the tool carefully along the rest without advancing it any further into the wood. The sideways movement must be slow in order to avoid cutting any identifiable grooves; this is best achieved by holding the tool firmly with an underhand grip for the steadying hand. The side of the index finger now rests firmly against the front face of the tool-rest to position and guide the cut, and particularly to control the depth.

Continue cutting until you have removed a depth of about ½in (13mm). At this stage you can see that the shadow image cut has just reached the bottom of the cove. Stop the lathe and check. You should now have untouched coves on one diagonal, but have just cut one wall of the cove right away at the centre.

FINISHING

A scraper is used to remove the small grooves left by the gouge. Remember always that a scraper is still a fine cutting tool and is used to take off tiny feathers of

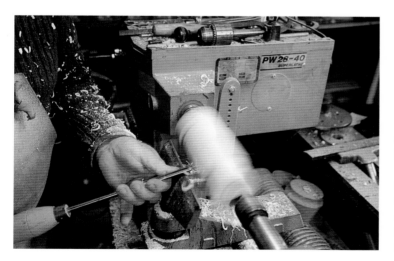

Fig. 106 Off-centre turning to create an oval column. The picture gives some idea of the shadowy edge image with which you have to work. It is just possible to detect the developing profile by closely watching the top edge.

wood to produce a smooth face. The best scraper for finishing a straight surface is a large, slightly rounded, 'dome' scraper; a 2in (5cm) dome is ideal. You do not use a square-ended scraper on flat surfaces, as this might itself leave edge marks.

Lower the tool-rest so that the cutting edge of the scraper is just below the height of the turning axis. The tool is held at right-angles to the axis and is moved very slowly and gently. Obviously you are still working into a shadowy image, and any misplacing of the blade will result in you catching a wing of the spindle.

You can either do the final finishing of the worked face now, or wait until the second side has been cut. Obviously final finishing is done by hand-sanding along the grain, but you will find that a power file sander is very useful in both finely shaping and initially finishing several forms of off-set work.

Unclamp, and then remount the spindle on the other pair of off-set centres. This should present the opposite face of the piece to the tool-rest, so you can repeat the cutting

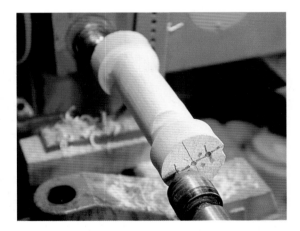

Fig. 107 The oval has been cut and now requires (hand-) finishing. Note the three turning axis points on the tailstock end. The centre axis is used to rough to a round and produce the end rings, and the two off-set are needed for the oval.

and finishing process. Again, stop when the centre of the cove has just been cut away.

You will have produced a spindle with round sections at each end, then partially cut-away coves, while the middle section is a true oval.

FURTHER INTERESTING EFFECTS

There are other experiments that you can now do. Start by cutting a little deeper towards one end of the spindle, and watch what this does to the shape of the oval. At the other end, see what happens if you slightly increase the off-set of the second and third pairs of centres. It is possible to achieve anything from a true oval to a round with two slightly flattened curved surfaces.

Another interesting effect can be produced by using five rather than three centres, giving a rounded square centre section.

An off-set centre effectively increases the radius of the timber, and therefore creates a flatter arc to the surface – the greater the off-set, the flatter the arc.

Of course, instead of turning a surface that is straight from end to end, you can cut a shallow concave. Cut the concave deeper until you cross the true centre, and the spindle will taper into a narrower waist. If you now remount the spindle on the opposite set of off-sets, and this time produce a long convex surface by turning away only the ends, you will produce a very stretched S profile.

Even with such a simple approach using ordinary drive spurs, and off-set but coincident centres, many interesting shapes can be produced. If non-coincident centres are used, even more complex designs are possible. Using a true centre and two pairs of diagonally opposed centres, interesting furniture legs with bun feet are possible.

MAKING AN OFF-SET BUD VASE

Before you get too ambitious, try another interesting piece. You will need a glass bud vase insert tube of ½in (13mm) external diameter, and a round section of timber of about 4in (10cm) in diameter and 12in (30cm) long. Mark each end of the wood with two centres, one the true centre which was used to round the spindle, and the other off-set by 1in (2.5cm). Using a pillar drill and a saw-tooth bit drill of the appropriate diameter, drill a hole in the top off-set centre to accept the full depth of the bud vase tube. Turn a small plug to fit the drilled hole, and indent the outboard end of the plug for the tailstock point.

Mount the timber on the lathe using the true centres, and round over the inboard end to produce the base of a bun-shaped foot.

Remount the piece on the lathe using the off-set centres, this time engaging the plug with the tailstock point. Turn the neck of the vase from this mounting, and fair the neck into the bun foot base. A little hand-working will be required to round off the top of the bun and achieve a good finish.

OFF-SET CHUCKS

Of course you are not totally confined in off-set turning by the diameter of the round blank. By gluing a wider disc on each end of the spindle you can also use centres that are outside the width of the blank. What we were doing in the oval exercise was to move the position of the surface of part of the circumference of the wood in respect of its presentation at the tool-rest: the wood was being rotated around the axis of the lathe but not around its own turning axis.

In making the bud vase we were spinning the wood around an axis within the wood which is now coincident with the lathe's axis. We did, however, move the position of the axis within the wood.

There are various ways that this can be done, and many turners have made up their own off-set chucks. Some of the DIY devices are fine and are relatively easy to operate, but some are on the verge of the Heath Robinson, and some are positively dangerous. Fortunately there are now commercially produced chucks available which simplify the whole process.

WHAT THEY ARE

Let us first clarify the principles. When turning wood on a lathe, the spindle (or bowl) spins around its axis. As we have just seen, this axis may be in the centre of the wood, or off-set to some degree. Whatever the level of off-set, the wood still turns – spins – around the axis of the lathe.

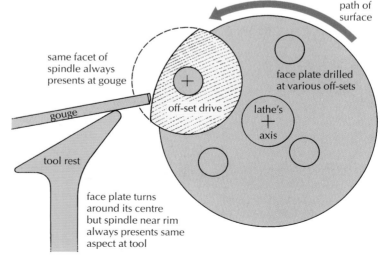

Fig. 108 Off-set turning on off-set axis.

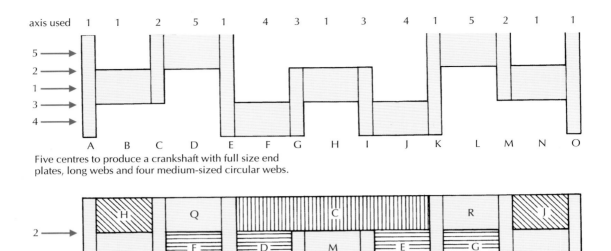

Five centres to produce a crankshaft with full size end plates, long webs and four medium-sized circular webs.

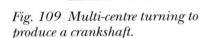

Fig. 109 Multi-centre turning to produce a crankshaft.

1. Rough spindle to a round on axis 1. Smooth.
2. Mount on axis 2 and remove shaded areas A and B.
3. Mount on axis 3 and rounding zone remove C.
4. Mount on axis 4 and round zones N and P by removing D and E.
5. Mount on axis 5 and round zones Q and R removing F and G.
6. Remount on axis 1 and remove zone K. Now fit a long steady on centre bearing M. Now work away H and J to fashion outermost con rod bearings. This leaves all the webs as turned in steps 1, 2 and 3.

If we were now to fix a wooden disc onto the face plate of the lathe and drill a hole into that disc at some point out towards its outer rim, and glue a spindle into that hole, the spindle would no longer rotate around its own axis – it would not spin, but it would circle around the axis of the face plate. It would be the same arc of the surface of the spindle that would be facing out at all times.

HOW TO USE THEM

If we now brought up a tool-rest and started to work on the spindle, we would always be cutting the same part of the spindle's face: we could, in fact, cut deep grooves into the outward-facing side of the spindle, while leaving the inner face untouched.

It is easy to see what is happening when you see an off-centre chuck in reality, but as turners are used to things spinning around their own axis, it is hard to get the mind around this aspect in abstract; it does require adopting a new 'mind-set' if we are to grasp the potential of off-centre chucking.

When you get down to it, it is quite easy to cut a crankshaft. For a model, think about a three-bearing crankshaft for an early make of four-cylinder car. At first sight you wonder how anybody could turn the inside face of the journal on 'the far side' of the crank. However, once you can divorce your mind from the concept of things being turned around (spun on) the lathe's axis, but can focus *only* upon the object being turned around the axis of the round element that you are looking at *at that moment*, you will see how a crankshaft might be turned.

In fact the piece is turned using three widely spaced centres. The first is the true centre, and from here the main spindle is turned (axis 1 on the diagram). The two end plates are to the full diameter of the basic spindle. From the same centres the webs E and K that flank the two centre con rod bearings are turned. The reduced diameters for the two end con rod bearings and the centre main bearing are also turned from the centre.

The spindle now has to be remounted on centres 2 and then 3 for the intermediate webs C and M, and then G and I to be fashioned. Axis 4 and its opposite axis 5 are used for turning the final off-set bearings; first F and J from 4; and D and L from axis 5.

Unfortunately, by now the piece is vibration prone and there are few suitable points for the mounting of a long work steady – just be careful, and 'Hey presto!' you have a replacement crank shaft for your old Austin 7!

MULTI-CENTRE TURNING

Keep the crankshaft in mind where each element is turned around its own central axis, and combine this with the idea of off-setting around either side of a turning axis: now the round could be made into ovals, and we are well on the way to an attractive and most interesting column for a table lamp. Obviously to make this we would now be working to axes 1, 2 and 3, and to two off-sets on each side of each of these. With the base central axis we could now have up to seven sets of turning axes, each being worked in turn.

From here the scope is open-ended. Instead of having axes 2 and 3 simply diametrically opposite, how about having four on the quadrants of the circle? In no time we get to the stage where the 'conrod journals' could spiral up the column. Further, instead of only two off-sets for each axis we could have three, and now the 'bearings' are rounded triangles in cross-section (just like my old cars were!).

There are limiting factors. First, just how much time you want to spend in calculating and setting up multiple centres and offsets. Secondly, if the 'crank' is too deep you could be compressing the spindle from the end plates and having to sustain the force

through a thin web with no through-section of timber grain; consequently the structure could easily become too fragile to drive. A third problem comes when you try to ovalize the faces of a cranked spindle. While turning the three main axes the crank is spinning around one or other of the axes, and the whole body remains within a reasonable overall turning circle. At some stage in each ovalizing, the main body of the spindle will be whirling round a very large turning circle.

ACHIEVING MULTIPLE OFF-SET CHUCKING

So much for the theory and some experimental methods; now let us look at the practical elements, and just how multiple off-set chucking can be achieved.

First, one problem that no turner appears to have solved is how to use the lathe to produce the beautiful compound curved legs with bun or ball and claw feet so favoured by Chippendale. The difficulty is not so much the continuous taper, but that there is also a continuous curve. The fact that the inside is often flat is no problem; what we cannot do is to turn with what is, in effect, a moving centre axis (this is where the fully automatic, computer controlled copy machines really score!).

Ian Durrant came near to it, followed soon after by Robert Sorby. It is also possible that somewhere in the complete kit that goes with the Holtzapfel lathe there is a gearing system that might produce the required effects. Basically what is required for off-set chucking is a face-plate chuck which fits onto the normal lathe's centre drive. There then has to be a means of fixing the end of the spindle somewhere on the face plate at various distances out from the centre axis.

The very crudest of arrangements is a face plate with a series of screw holes drilled at various distances from the centre. The spindle to be turned is then fixed end-on to

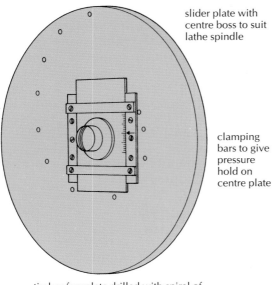

slider plate with
centre boss to suit
lathe spindle

clamping
bars to give
pressure
hold on
centre plate

timber faceplate drilled with spiral of
holes to through screw to hold spindle

Fig. 110 A DIY chuck for off-set turning.

the face plate, and is held in position by a screw through the plate. In a simple DIY device, such as is shown in the diagram a sliding 'screw chuck' can be moved to provide infinitely variable degrees of off-set.

The problem with both of these approaches is that it is difficult to reposition (partially rotate) the spindle on the screw chuck. Hence while they will effectively produce either a single off-set, as in the drilled face plate, or degrees of off-set in the same plane as the variable mounting unit, they will not lend themselves to producing controllable, sophisticated, multi-angled pieces.

THE OCA OFF-CENTRE CHUCK

The OCA off-centre chuck is Ian Durrant's brainchild. Ian is a well-known turner who has won many competitions not only for his innovative off-centre turnings, but also for many of his 'straight' pieces which are executed to the finest designs and the

highest standards of finish. After some years of experimentation he produced his 'OCA' Offset Chuck Adapter. This consists of a small face plate which is tapped out with nine holes set in a spiral; into the holes may be screwed a threaded spigot or 'Stud' onto the outboard end of which may be fixed the lathe's normal chuck.

The spiral of holes allows offsets of ¼, ⅝, ¾, ⅞, 1, 1¼, 1⅜, and 1⅝in (5, 15, 18, 20, 23, 25, 30, 35 and 40mm). Ian spent many hours in advanced mathematical calculations, on the drawing board and in the workshop in establishing that these levels of off-set gave the most useful possibilities.

The OCA kit is a relatively simple and inexpensive unit which is available to fit most standard lathes. It is provided with a drilled face plate to fit directly onto the turner's lathe, and with a spigot threaded at one end to fit the holes in the face plate, and at the other end to the normal size of the lathe's spindle. This means that it may be used with whatever chucking device (s) the turner has available (multi, collet, screw, dovetail and so on). There is also a spigot with a cross-head drive end.

THE SORBY RS60 ECCENTRIC CHUCK

Robert Sorby in their RS60 Eccentric Chuck have gone for a more sophisticated approach. Their kit consists of a beautifully presented standard package with a number of driving devices and adapters. There is then a screw-in adapter to fit the user's particular lathe. The work is normally held on the chuck with a beefy 1in by ⅜in (25 by 10mm) parallel wood screw, although a small face plate and other drives are included. There are also adapters to allow the unit to be used with Sorby's own Premier chuck, so spigot or collet options are available through this extra. The standard screw is fixed in a rotating mount within the chuck body, and this allows infinitely variable levels of off-set from 0 to 1¼in (0 to 30mm).

Fig. 111 Two off-set chucking aids. To the left is Ian Durrant's simple but effective OCA unit. Your normal chuck screws onto the plug. In the case is the more sophisticated Sorby unit which includes an angle-driving socket.

(Below) Fig. 112 The Sorby unit set-up with a screw chuck. The off-set is continuously variable.

INDEXING DEVICES

It is useful, although not essential, to use an off-centre chuck with some form of indexing device. You don't need the accuracy of a pin-clamped forty-eight-hole head but the facility to be able to control both the level of off-set and the arc of the axis of the spindle that is being cut does extend the possibilities. An indexing head, and a variable degree of off-set, plus the ability to be able to rotate the spindle easily to fixed positions on or in its mountings, makes the working of the spiralling crankshaft suggested earlier relatively easy.

Both chucks allow for indexing the wood on its mounting, and for off-setting at the drive end while using true centres at the tailstock.

Fig. 113 Ian Durrant starts one of his fine goblets. The small bowl is finished and plugged for support.

The outer rim of Ian Durrant's OCA is marked off to provide twelve indexing positions. The base of the piece being turned (usually a waste mounting block) is marked with a zero line – a pencil mark on a piece of masking tape is sufficient. The piece can then be rotated by slackening off the collet grip, and reclamped against an index mark on the OCA's body. This allows infinitely variable possibilities.

The Sorby device also has indexing marks on the rim, and the screw drive can be notched around within a twelve-point socket.

Fig. 114 What off-set multi-centre turning can really look like. A display of Ian Durrant's work.

CONCLUSION

For safety, off-centre turning is done at slow lathe speeds, and this in turn means that tools should be kept extremely sharp. Whereas most of us grind our tools on 80- to 100-grit wheels, Ian's standard is 200. Ian also recommends that 500rpm should be considered as being the very top speed for a 2in (5cm) diameter piece.

However, as our first experiment indicated, you don't need any device to start with: just a good drive centre, a pencil and ruler,

Fig. 115 Captive rings cut with the special Sorby scrapers.

and above all, a lot of imagination. Even when you read the manuals supplied with the proprietary chucks you will not really see the scope and possibilities – you just have to experiment for yourself. Try both multi-centre and off-set centre turning; initially treat them as two separate subjects until you fully understand what is going on, and *then* start to combine them! One thing is for certain, and that is you will get many questions such as, 'Just *how* did you do that?'

14

A LATHE IS NOT THE ONLY ANSWER

The one problem with lathes is that they only turn round things! Even the decoration that you apply can really only go around the circumference whether it is true, oval, faceted or off-set; so what can you do when you want decoration that runs along the axis of the spindle?

There is something to be said for longitudinal decoration to break up or off-set the continual roundness, and in a way, square sections do this. Certainly they provide a nice contrast to circular decoration. Designers have long found that the introduction of decoration such as fluting and reeds along the axis gives considerable eye appeal; both these and spirals, as in rope and barley twist, assist the eye to make relatively fast journeys from end to end.

DEVELOPMENT IN CHAIR LEG DESIGN

It is very difficult to date accurately the developments in chair leg design, but the sequence broadly went from whole board to spaced square section and then to turned; from turned it went to curved and to turned fluted, then to spirals and barley twist. At various stages and under different influences there have been switches back and forth between squared and rounded section.

So legs have been variously totally unturned, totally turned, and turned with unturned carved and incised decoration. They have also been turned between true centres and between off-set centres. The history has been one of constant change and variety. Clearly in this text we are concerned with those approaches where the leg has been turned on the lathe at some stage – but not necessarily throughout.

In the past, non-turned decoration was applied with other traditional carpentry and cabinet-making methods. As we have seen, barley-twist legs were turned to cylinders, and then the spirals were cut with hand-saw, chisels and gouges. Fluting was done by first turning the round sections of the leg, and then incising the pattern with fine moulding planes, or more frequently with scratch stocks. Some of the square-section, fine tapered legs of the Regency period only saw a lathe for a few brief instants while some small circular decoration was applied.

DEVELOPMENTS IN MACHINERY AND TOOLING

Today, extensive use is made of machines. In volume production the automatic copy lathes referred to earlier have power cutters – usually routers – which can be set to incise circular decoration, but which can also cut spirals and lateral fluting patterns.

Inventive small shop craftsmen have developed a number of less expensive alternatives. In looking at them here we will cover some of the more widely developed ideas; although this will be done not so much to provide a definitive list of options, but rather to explore some of the things that can and already have been done and, hopefully, to stimulate other turners into developing new ideas for themselves.

It is worthwhile emphasizing that almost every development in the machinery and tooling used in turning has *not* been the product of a design studio or an all-purpose inventor; nor has it even emanated originally from the design rooms of the larger machinery or tool manufacturers. Rather, these advances have come from working turners who were faced with a problem, and who then designed their own solution for it; it was only after the craftsmen had introduced the device into their own workshops that the manufacturers came along and either bought, adapted or sometimes stole the ideas.

As an aside, it has to be noted that most manufacturers are always looking out for ideas that can be developed and marketed. They, of course, have the facilities, the know-how and the *entrées* to markets that are not readily available to the inventive craftsman. It also needs to be recorded that the greatest care has to be taken when entering into contractual relationships. Some companies are extremely good, whilst others – including some high profile organizations – have been very unfair (and in a few cases verging on the crooked) with the original designers.

The problem with trying to work decoration along the axis of the spindle is the minimum speed at which the lathe will turn. Obviously with true straight-along-the-axis decoration you don't want the lathe turning at all. As was suggested earlier, the machine-cutting of spirals requires that there is a synchronization between the speed of lathe rotation and the speed that the tool travels along the axis, and this just cannot be achieved manually. For this reason spirals have to be cut on special lathes, or to be hand-carved with gouges.

Straight axial decoration can still use the lathe – in fact it is the best possible 'vice' for holding the workpiece while the carving is being executed. What is more, the lathe also provides the best means of spacing, both accurately and equally, the decoration around the spindle.

INDEXING HEADS

Fundamental to most lateral decoration is an indexing head to control the spacing. Some lathes are supplied with an indexer; many are not. A few of those that come as a standard part of the basic lathe are satisfactory; but again, many are not.

An indexing head provides a means of locking the lathe's drive spindle in fixed positions at set intervals around the circumference of the turning circle. In its basic form it consists of a pin that drops into equally spaced holes on a ring around the drive spindle to prevent rotation. The ring of marks or holes is sometimes cut into one of the drive pulleys on the lathe spindle, and the pin pivots off the head casing. On other lathes the circle of holes is drilled into a ring on the outboard end of the drive spindle.

NON-PROPRIETARY RINGS

Where the lathe does not have an indexer there are non-proprietary rings available which clamp onto some of the more widely used patterns of chuck. Many turners have made their own rings. There are two essentials: first, that the ring or scale locks onto or is an integral part of the drive spindle; and the other is that the pin does lock the spindle and will hold it tight while work is being done on the piece.

One of two hole-spacing patterns are used on the rings: one has a twelve base, and the other a ten base. The twelve-base hole spacing is the more common, and while there are a few heads with only twelve

Fig. 116 The indexer fitted as standard to the Poolewood lathe.

Fig. 117 An old piano leg, probably cut with a scratch stock. Two home-made stocks are also shown with bits of hacksaw blades ground to provide cutters.

equally spaced holes, there are more with twenty-four. The best models have a full forty-eight holes, and these are the most practical. The ten-base spacing is most frequently found as a sixty-hole ring. If used as a basis for fluting, a forty-eight-hole ring would allow you to cut two flutes on opposite sides of the circumference, four on quarters, or equally spaced combinations of two, three, four, six, eight, twelve, sixteen, twenty-four or forty-eight.

A sixty-hole ring provides two, three, four, five, six, ten, twelve, fifteen, twenty, thirty and sixty positions for flutes, but some turners find sixty holes, with their close spacing, are just too many to be practical.

THE CUTTING OF FLUTES

The actual cutting of flutes can be done in three ways. The most difficult and rarely used is a moulding plane with an appropriately profiled blade. The second, the traditional method, uses a scratch stock; and the third is a router. In the past all were used in conjunction with a box or cradle.

SCRATCH STOCKS

Scratch stocks are made by the user, and are extremely simple and quite effective. In essence they consist of a handle into which is clamped a steel scraper. Today, most craftsmen profile their own scrapers from broken lengths of hacksaw blade.

A good stock handle can be made from two 'L' shaped pieces of hardwood (beech or oak) which are screwed together. The screws on the long arm of the L are eased so that the hacksaw blade can be pushed through in the working position and then the screws pinched up. The cutting location is controlled by the distance of the blade from the foot of the L, and the depth of penetration controlled by the amount of blade that is showing. The blade can be profiled on the corner of the wheel of a grinder, and may be dressed with a round diamond lap.

Fig. 118 The beading and the rule joint on this table top were cut with a larger size scratchstock.

The foot of the L is kept in contact with the side of the timber being decorated and the stock is pushed or pulled along according to the lie of the grain.

Quite sizeable decoration can be produced with a scratch stock such as the edge beading and chamfers on table tops and the rule joint on drop-leaf tables.

Techniques and Problems

To scratch flutes or reeds down the length of a leg, the leg is turned to a straight or tapered cylinder and is then left on the lathe and the position fixed by the indexing head. An open-top box is made which clamps to the lathe bed and which 'cradles' the workpiece. The stock is now worked along the open top of the box with the foot of the L over the side to keep the run true. The blade is positioned to groove the apex of the workpiece.

Fortunately we usually only cut fine flutes in beech, mahogany and walnut (woods which are fine grained and not too dense), and scratch stocks are quite effective on these timbers. They do not, however, like oak, elm or pine, blunting very quickly on oak, being thrown by the wild grain in elm, and to some extent tearing the fibres in pine. They also work well in the fine-grained, harder exotic timbers such as rosewoods and bubinga – provided you are prepared to spend time keeping the scratch stock cutter sharp.

One thing that the cutting of fluting does quickly reveal is how true is the taper on the spindle you are decorating – and how true are the top edges of the cradle box. If the taper is good, the flutes will have an even profile; if not, then you get some with flat tops and some with little peaks, or a varying width of spacing shoulders.

It is possible to scratch (or route) a curved leg where the curve has either a gentle concave or convex profile. It is, however quite difficult to shape the top edge of the box to match the profile of the spindle exactly.

Should you be contemplating regular work of this nature, it is worth making a basic box which has true top edges. It is made so that its mounting to the lathe can be adjusted for various diameters of spindle and various pitches of slope. Profile boards can then be made, which clamp by way of coach bolts and wing nuts in slotted holes to the sides of the box. A template is made of the profile boards, and the spindle is turned to match the template accurately.

METHODS USING A ROUTER

Today, except in a few traditionalist workshops or for a one-off job, routers have replaced scratch stocks. Let us look at some of the router approaches to fluting.

The first of the routing methods uses similar mounting methods to the moulding plane and scratch stock. Again a cradle box is clamped to the lathe bed, but here, instead of the stock, you run the router along the top of the box using the router fence over the edge to control the trueness of the run.

An interesting alternative uses a system developed by Tony Bunce of Techlink Enterprises Limited; as an idea it is so obvious that others must have come up with similar devices. Another method uses a piece of equipment now marketed by Trend as the 'Routerlathe' (*see* Chapter 15). Again, from articles appearing in the woodworking press over the years, it is obvious that several turners have made similar units of their own.

The Techlink System

The full Techlink kit consists of two parts: an indexing head system which is made to fit whichever chuck you normally use; and then a mounting block that will take a medium-power router or a die-grinder. The unit – in fact the complete kit – is very simple in concept and design (as the best ideas often are); but what makes it so effective and useful are the simple mounting systems which Tony has designed, and which allow it to cut controlled arcs and complex profiles.

The mounting block has a vertical arm with a clamp to fit the standard 1¾in (43mm) router collar; the clamp can be positioned anywhere up the vertical to allow for different over-bed heights of lathe. The foot of the unit is polished to slide on an MDF bed-plate clamped to the top of the lathe bed. The router can be used totally 'freehand', if required, by gripping the unit firmly in both hands and sliding it over the bed-board.

Controlling the Movement

There are two means of controlling the movement: the first uses an arm and pivot pin block, and the second uses shaped templates. With the block system, the arm passes through the body of the router bracket running from front to back, and it can be locked in any required position. At the end of the arm are slots to fit over the pin on the pivot block. The length of arm left projecting obviously governs the arc of swing. The block itself is fixed on the base-board with a hexagonal bolt and wing nut. When the pivot pin is mounted in front of the router, the head will swing in a concave arc enabling the cutter to

Fig. 119 (Top) The Techlink system here using a die-grinder, but the column will accept standard medium routers. The screws at the bottom of the block run against the template, here a piece of aluminium clamped to the base board. The indexer is holding the spindle locked.
(Bottom) The router is pushed by hand, starting from the outboard end.

swing round the face of a convex surface such as the outside wall of a bowl. Mount the pivot pin to the rear, and the cutter describes a convex arc, hence cutting on a concave surface.

The swing arm has a slotted hole to fit over the pivot pin. This governs (and limits)

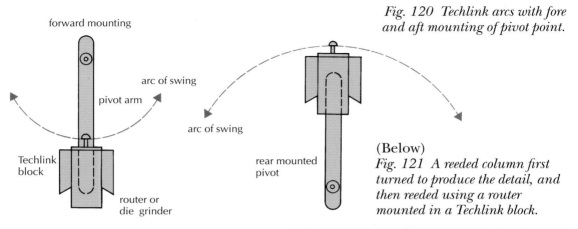

Fig. 120 Techlink arcs with fore and aft mounting of pivot point.

forward mounting

arc of swing

pivot arm

Techlink block

router or die grinder

arc of swing

rear mounted pivot

(Below)
Fig. 121 A reeded column first turned to produce the detail, and then reeded using a router mounted in a Techlink block.

the depth of cut. The tool is positioned with the pivot block slackened a little. The block is moved until the cutter describes an arc which follows precisely the contour to be grooved – with the unit drawn back in the slot to pin coupling. The block is then clamped off. The router is started and pushed forwards on the slot and then moved in the controlled arc. In other words the slot provides a controlled 'plunge'.

Using Templates
The second means of governing the sweep is to use templates. A plate (usually a large piece of MDF) of the required profile is clamped to the top of the base-board, and the router unit is pushed against this. There are two round-headed screws on the front of the router bracket, and it is the heads of these that are held in contact with the template. The screws are easily adjusted so that again, the router and template can be set to sweep just clear of the surface to be cut, and then the screws can be taken down to give the required depth of cut.

Routing Flutes along a Spindle's Axis
To rout flutes along the axis of a spindle you now have two basic options: one is the cradle box, as with the scratch stock method, where the router may be run down the top of the spindle. The second is to mount the router in or on a block so that the machine is horizontal and the block is then held down onto a base-board. In both cases it is normal to make the cuts coincide closely with the central axis of the spindle. If not, then the cut will be off-set and the flute will not have a symmetrical profile.

Obviously the spindle has to be locked in position for each sweep of the router –

hence the need for a good index head locking system – and the router needs to run on or against a guide.

For straight taper legs, the guide for the side-block cutting is a simple straight-edge clamped to the bed-board. Of course it must be of sufficient thickness to engage the heads of the running screws; and it has to be both cut and mounted so that it is absolutely true to the surface of the spindle.

Important Operational Points

There are certain vital operational points. The entry and the length of the cut should be made in one continuous, slow sweep. You may, of course, have to make more than one pass in order to achieve the full depth of cut required. Cutting too deep or putting any form of pressure on the cutter is likely to result in a torn surface. The entry should not be started until the router is running at full speed, and it should *always start at the outboard end*. This is essential because of the direction of rotation of the cutter. As seen from the front face the cutter is rotating anti-clockwise. If the cutter is swept from left to right (inboard to outboard ends) it tends to climb up the front of the cut: this will either pull the router away from the operator if the machine is making a vertical pass as on the box cradle; or it will lift up off the table if the router is working horizontally as in a bracket mount. You can hold the router unit as firmly as you like, but a slight variation in wood or a moment's inattention, and the groove you are cutting will have waves – or worse. So always sweep from right to left!

PATTERNS OF FLUTING

There are normally two patterns of fluting (as distinct from spirals and twists) applied to spindles: one is either a rounded-over or pyramid form reeding; and the other a cove or grooving. Most commonly both adopt the semicircular profile, although vee- or square-section grooves are sometimes used. Issues such as finishing and cleaning may have influenced the conventions but there is no reason why you should not experiment with various patterns.

Whatever you do, you will be faced with an immediate choice. The decoration may be such that there is a flat zone between each reed or flute, although the convention – and a much neater and more satisfying arrangement – is to have one reed flowing immediately into the next in a continuous wave form. With grooves however, a narrow flat shoulder between each groove is more appropriate, because the sharp peak created by merging two parallel grooves will break out and catch dresses and stockings.

The structural requirements for the spindle that you are making will largely determine its overall diameter. Most frequently your design will require that the reeded or fluted section is tapered – it may even be an ogee compound curve.

GROOVED PATTERNS

With grooved patterns, anything but a parallel walled cylinder can present some difficulties. If the groove remains a constant width and depth throughout its length, then the width of the flat shoulder between adjacent grooves will vary according to the diameter of the spindle at that point. At best on a taper the shoulder will itself be a long wedge shape, possibly disappearing altogether at the narrow end. The alternative is to set the template or straight-edge such that the router cuts slightly less deep towards the end – this will have the effect of making the groove progressively less deep and slightly narrower. Both tapered and parallel shoulders are therefore possible. Some turners think that tapering shoulders add to the effect and perspective of the fluting.

With both grooved and reeded forms, the diameter of the spindle must condition

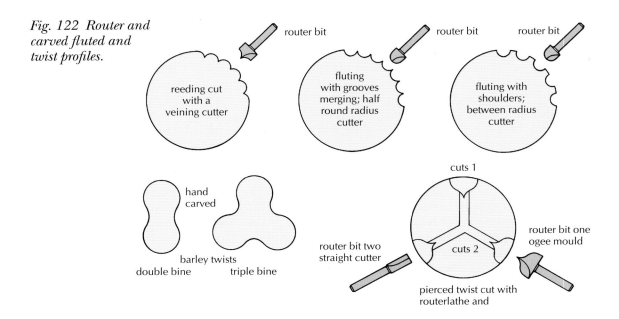

Fig. 122 Router and carved fluted and twist profiles.

the width of the decorative element, and obviously the required width will determine the size of cutter used. This, in turn, will influence the number of grooves or reeds around the diameter of the spindle. Fluted chair legs typically have a maximum diameter of around 2⅜in (6cm) and taper down to about 1¾in (4.5cm). If a 2in (5cm) diameter spindle were given twelve grooves/reeds, each would be a fraction over ½in (13mm) wide – and this would appear chunky. A better arrangement would be eighteen grooves or reeds each just under ⅜in (9mm) wide.

A 3in (7.5cm) wide spindle – and this is a typical diameter for a fluted table leg – would have twelve flutes of just over ¾in (20mm) wide, which is again much too big, or eighteen of ½in (13mm) plus.

If you look at the router bit catalogues of the main suppliers you will find that the round-nose bits (or radius cutters) which are used to produce grooves or coves, progress in ⅛in (3mm) increments from ⅛in (3mm) to ½in (13mm); then in ¼in (6mm) increments to 1¼in (32mm). There are then larger guttering cutters for fluting bigger diameter columns. All are half-round, producing a nice, even semicircular groove. So by choice of cutter, and choosing an appropriate hole spacing on the indexer, it is possible to adjust the grooves to suit the diameter and proportions of the leg that you are working on.

REEDED PATTERNS

Reeding is obviously achieved by cutting valleys so that only the apex of the 'ridge' remains at the full diameter of the spindle. Here we look to panelling, veining or ovolo cutters. Unfortunately the size range in those with a fine centre point is much more limited, ⅜ and ½in (9.5 and 13mm) being the most widely available.

There are many profiles that can be used with larger diameter spindles and columns, and a router may even be set up to cut on the top of a spindle using a horizontal corner bead cutter. In fact with the vast range of cutters now available and a little imagination, some quite exciting possibilities exist.

BASE-BOARD MOUNTED ROUTERS

Base-board mounted routers offer another range of possibilities – just consider what happens if you tilt the base-board. The board usually used with the Techlink is made by the turner of the thicker grade of MDF to suit their own requirements. Often it is a table which fits between the head-stock block and the tailstock block, the table being probably four times the width of the lathe bed. The width is required so that the pivot pin can be placed to give very wide swings (gentle arcs).

To accommodate spindles of different lengths the board is slotted at the outboard end to allow the tailstock to be brought in. The basic board is drilled with ¼in (6mm) diameter holes on a 2 × 2in (5 × 5cm) grid pattern; this, coupled with the slot in the top of the pivot block and the adjustment available in the clamping of the swing arm, means that the pin may be located absolutely anywhere on the board, giving an infinitely variable degree of cutting arc. The board is normally clamped or bolted flat to the lathe bed.

METHODS OF WORKING

If the front end of the board is fixed to the lathe bed, but the outboard end is blocked up an inch or two, the grooves that the router cuts will obviously be inclined to the axis of the spindle. With this arrangement the router is usually mounted in the bracket such that it starts cutting above axis height; at the middle of the cut it is level with the axis and then as the router sweeps on towards the headstock, the cut falls below the axis. Obviously the cut should be a concave sweep, and by juggling the arc and incline, it is possible to cut tear-drop and other scooping and scalloped grooves.

The inclined table really comes into its own when turning lamp bases (and of course bowls) on the face plate, when a huge variety of inclined and spiralling designs can be worked.

Using the Board with a Template

To use the board with a template means first cutting the template in MDF and clamping this to the base-board. A set of templates of various radii can be produced with simple curves, both symmetrical and hyperbolic; with a little juggling, these can be positioned and then bolted to the base-board to suit almost any single curve. Compound curves such as ogees do give difficulties, however. Parallax errors, and the different distances of the template tracking point and cutter tip from the lathe's axis, mean that you are on different arcs and so the template cannot therefore mirror the profile of the piece.

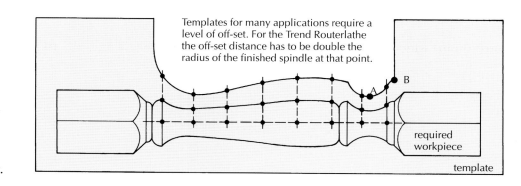

Fig. 123 Drawing templates.

Templates for many applications require a level of off-set. For the Trend Routerlathe the off-set distance has to be double the radius of the finished spindle at that point.

required workpiece

template

143

MAKING COPIES

It is a matter of pride to most spindle turners that they will cut all the circumferential detail on the spindle using traditional turning techniques. This is not now absolutely necessary, however, since any profile that can be cut with skews and gouges can equally well be cut with a router. This is, in effect, what the high quality copy lathes do.

Most cradle boxes for the router cutting of reeds and flutes can only be used with the lathe static. The base-board and bracket-mounted routers can be used with the spindle turning, either being rotated by hand or with the lathe running at the lowest speed.

Here again, the Techlink type mounting is useful. The router is clamped in the bracket so that it is aligned with the centre axis of the spindle. The lathe is started and then the router, and keeping the router at right-angles to the spindle axis, it is advanced very slowly into the workpiece. Hold the bracket with both hands, with the heel of the hand pressing down on the base-board; this prevents the router from kicking sideways and ensures a nice crisp cut. To make very accurate copies you need only to mark off the position of each detail on the base-board and you can always clamp on a bar to act as a backstop and prevent cutting too deep.

The diagram shows the different cuts and identifies the appropriate Trend cutter for each.

THE DISADVANTAGES OF FREEHAND ROUTER-CUTTING

While you can produce circular decorated spindles using a router in this way, you will probably find that it is not a worthwhile process. Freehand router-cutting is not easy, and with the lathe turning, even at a slow speed, it is extremely difficult to achieve any level of accuracy. What is more, it takes very much longer to stop the router, remove the cutter, find and fit the next cutter and then start up again, than it does merely to pick up the next turning tool and make a proper cut. Using hand-held routers is not a half-way stage between turning-tool cutting and fully automatic router-cutting lathes.

There is a better router alternative, however, and that is to use the Trend Router-lathe; this provides the subject of our next chapter. Unfortunately the remarks about cutter changing time against using conventional turning tools still hold.

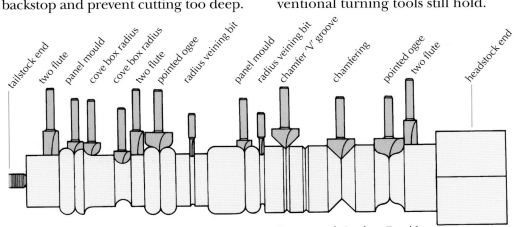

Fig. 124 Decorating spindles with a router.

Recommendation from Trend for router bits to decorate spindles. The pierced twist uses the pointed ogee and a long thin straight two flute.

15

THE ROUTERLATHE

If your business is making and selling router cutters, then you will obviously be interested in promoting anything that will advance routing. Thus, over the years Trend, who must make some of the world's best router bits, have also offered a number of router accessories. These include jig- and template-making systems; diamond sharpeners; the superb craftsman's level routing table with its huge range of accessories; and the unit which most concerns us here: the Routerlathe.

THE TREND ROUTERLATHE

The Trend Routerlathe is an interesting piece of kit that can be used to produce a range of twist, rope and fluted spindles. Over the years, and both before and after the introduction of the Trend unit, innovative craftsmen have produced their own devices all working on similar principles, and several of these have been described in the woodworking press. So the idea cannot be bad!

If you are interested in volume commercial work, then you too will have to go the DIY route, for Trend themselves make it clear that the Routerlathe is designed for hobby use. Perhaps they are being a little over-cautious, however.

The principle of all such machines is that there is a frame into which a spindle can be mounted. In the case of the Trend, it is a four-sided steel tube frame which can accommodate a spindle of up to 38in (93cm) in length and (3in) 7.6cm diameter. On this it can cut decoration to a maximum length of 26in (63cm). There then has to be a carriage which moves smoothly along the top of the frame, and this has to accept portable router

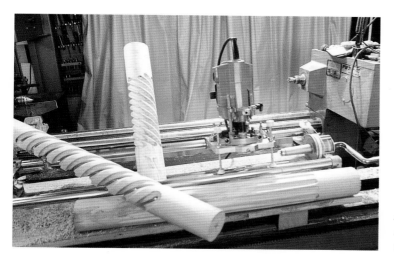

Fig. 125 The Trend Routerlathe with some of its products.

Fig. 126 Turning the end handle rotates the spindle and draws the router table along the track.

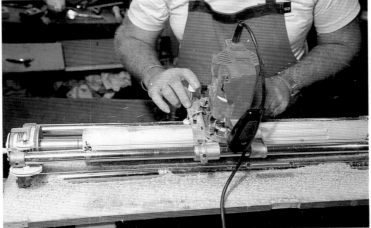

Fig. 127 To produce straight fluting the spindle is locked, the cable released, and the carriage moved by hand.

units. Again, the Trend will take almost any make of medium-powered routers of up to 1,100 watts and ¼in (6mm) bit capacity. The next requirement has to be a mechanism (usually a wire rope and pulleys) which turns the spindle and which directly links the rotation of the spindle with the travel of the router carriage. On the Routerlathe the linking mechanism can be disconnected and the spindle locked in a fixed position; the carriage can now be pushed by hand to cut straight reeds and flutes.

ITS LIMITATIONS

So why is the Trend Routerlathe said to be only a hobby-level tool? First, it will accept only medium-powered routers – although these are more than adequate for most work. The second limitation, and this is probably the most significant, is that there is only one gear available and hence it is not possible to vary the pitch of a spiralling twist. The third problem is that some elements are made to a hobby price – they are serviceable, but possibly not robust enough to withstand the abuses of a production environment. It must be remembered, however, that you are comparing a useful light unit with its nearest rival, and this is a full copy lathe with router cutting mechanisms at something like fifty times the price of the Routerlathe.

GOOD POINTS

There are many good points. First, the unit will accept both square or already rounded stock. Second, there is a very simple but totally effective indexing head device built in. Third, all the bits and brackets are supplied for fitting the machine to a bench or base-board, and for clamping on whatever router you have available. And fourth, there is the vast range of profiles of router bits available from Trend and other manufacturers.

MAKING TAPERS AND CURVED SHAPES

Of course many furniture legs are not straight, nor do all have simple straight tapers; many are curved, and a good router lathe must be able to accommodate both of these aspects. Dealing with tapers is simple, because all that is needed is to provide a means of raising or lowering the tailstock point. On the Routerlathe the point is set in an adjustable plate which is graduated to provide the required levels of off-set, and it is only a few seconds' job to make any necessary adjustment.

Dealing with curved shapes is not quite so easy. Here, as with most others, the Trend unit depends upon the use of templates. The front of the router carriage is provided with a tracing finger, and this can follow along the profile of the template. Unlike copy lathes where you would copy the full profile and all detail, it is a reasonable assumption that most turners would prefer to use their normal lathe to cut circular

decoration. Hence they would normally only wish to trace the broad profile of a leg when fluting with the Routerlathe.

There is still a problem, however, because the template cannot be cut to a mirror image of the silhouette of the pattern leg, and allowance has to be made for off-sets. The silhouette has to be traced out first, and the centre axis has to be drawn in. At key points along the profile the distance from the axis to the surface has to be measured, and this must then be doubled to find the tracing point for the template. This means that every curve is amplified (*see* Fig. 123).

SOME ISSUES OF USE

But let us get down to practicalities, and some of the issues of use. As normally supplied, the Routerlathe is set up for square stock and there are instructions for using the unit to turn this to round by making successive passes with a straight cutter. This is a long and tedious process, however, and would certainly accelerate the wearing of the machine (including the powered router head). Against this there is a little difficulty in using ready rounded stock. The Routerlathe's four-point centre has very fine points and it is not easy to locate these accurately into the indent left by a lathe's normal drive centre. The solution is not difficult, however: first, find the centre using diagonal lines, and then indent this first with the Routerlathe centre. Then using the marks, make an indent again with the normal spur. Error is very rare if done this way, as it is much easier and more accurate.

The importance of accuracy cannot be over-stressed, because if you are off centre, even by half a millimetre, this affects the depth of routing and the width of the shoulders between flutes, a discrepancy that becomes very evident when you look at the finished piece. Remember that the variation of depth in the flute will be twice the off-set error from one side of the spindle to the other.

Once double marked, the blank can be roughed to a round, any round-to-square junctions can be finished, and any circular decoration applied on a conventional lathe before the spindle is transferred to the Routerlathe. This is very much quicker. What is more, there are decorations that you can apply with ordinary turning tools that would require a comprehensive range of router bits, and router bits are *much* more expensive than lathe tools! Trend do, however, supply a quite useful kit of seven router bits specially selected for use with the Routerlathe, and these give several interesting possibilities.

While most profiles of bit are available in high speed steel or tungsten carbide, anyone who uses a router regularly will insist upon the more expensive carbide-tipped variety because they last many times longer. Even slightly worn or blunted bits are the quickest route to torn grain. Of course, bits can be sharpened provided you use a diamond lap or a greenstone on the rear (the vertical) face of the tungsten carbide insert – not on the bevel of the cutter profile.

SPIRALLING TWISTS AND STRAIGHT FLUTES

The first task in undertaking any spiralling twist or straight fluting work is to calculate the number of bines, or the spacing of the flutes.

CALCULATING THE NUMBER OF BINES OR FLUTES

With a pair of external callipers, measure the diameter of the round spindle that you are going to decorate. Convert this into a circumference by multiplying the diameter by 3.142. Next, measure the maximum diameter of the bit you propose to use. From this you can calculate the number of flutes that you could evenly space around the circumference, and you can also determine whether there needs to be a shoulder between each flute, and how wide the shoulder should be.

For instance, you have a spindle which is exactly 3in (7.6cm) in diameter. This gives a circumference of:

$$3 \times 3.142 = 9.426\text{in} \ (7.62\text{cm})$$

The fluting cutter that you are using has a diameter of ½in, or 0.5in (13mm) hence you could have:

$$9.426/0.5\text{in} = 18.85 \text{ flutes}$$
$$\text{(with no shoulders)}$$

Obviously you would round up to eighteen flutes. However, depending on the spacings and hole pattern of your indexing head you may not have eighteen evenly spaced settings available. If it is a forty-eight-hole head, the nearest you could achieve by rounding up would be sixteen; you would therefore be able to cut sixteen flutes each of ½in width and there would be a small shoulder (flat) of about one-twelfth of an inch between them (give or take a cutting error – and my poor maths!) Alternatively you could go for twenty-four index positions thereby merging each flute into the next.

As was mentioned in the notes on design, a small shoulder is better as it limits breakout and sharp edges if you are fluting coves. If, on the other hand, you are cutting rounded reeds, then rounding up to fewer reeds may result in each reed being slightly flat-topped; or rounding down (to twenty-four) might result in a slight pointing which could itself be rounded by turning the spindle against a light abrasive. In general, when calculating the number of flutes or reeds we round down.

THE SEQUENCE OF CUTTING

Once you have determined the number of flutes, or whatever, the next thing to decide is the sequence of cutting. Some patterns – such as through or pierced barley twist – are cut using more than one profile of bit. As a general principle it is better to work the shoulders – that is, the wider and shallower cuts – first, before plunging into the depths. Nor is it recommended that you try to achieve the full depth in one pass.

You do have two options. The first is to allow the machine to take charge and to find its own natural depth as it cuts; this way you have to make two or three passes before the router naturally bottoms out. This is too crude, however, and a controlled multi-pass process is to be preferred. The easiest method of approaching this is to pre-set the depth of cut to a half or one-third of the finished depth, and to cut all the flutes all the way round the cylinder before re-setting the router to make the second and deeper cut.

Cutting a pierced barley twist may require up to ten passes, but I find it to be still considerably quicker than by hand. You may need three passes to achieve the full depth of the shoulder form. In the example illustrated in Fig. 128 this involved a pointed ogee cutter (Trend pattern C142 from the basic kit); the through-cutting then used a long straight cutter (pattern C008, again from the basic kit). The shoulders took three passes, and then five passes took out and cleaned the deep channels. The last two passes were with slight sideways finger pressure against the router first one side, and then the other. The pressure took up slack in the mechanism and ensured even contact, with the side walls taking away intermediate cut depth marks. It must be noted, however, that any sideways finger pressure on the router can cause tracking misalignments and must be done with extreme care.

SOME BASIC RULES OF PRACTICE

One thing you learn very quickly with all routing approaches, and that is the importance of cutting in the right direction for the rotation of the router (against the direction of rotation). Always start the cut with the router at the outboard end, and *never* try to reverse the cut by making a return pass in the opposite direction. There is also sufficient inherent play in the Routerlathe drive mechanism to *ensure* that the reverse pass will not track the forward pass precisely.

There are other finer points of practice:

- Do not hold the router down and force it to cut – although on the final pass a little light finger pressure on the top will ensure an even depth throughout the pass.
- Never force the cutter along, but take it gently: the moment you put pressure on the handle and force the router to cut, you will get torn grain on even the most amenable of timbers.
- Always make each and every cut in one end-to-end pass. If you try to pick up in the middle of a cut, a small step *will* be created.
- Never let the router run in the same spot for any length of time as there is a risk of heat scorching the groove.
- Start the router before you lower it into its cutting position, and switch it off *before* lifting it from the groove. Wind the carriage back with the router stopped. When doing deep piercing, however, and when you are getting down towards the bottom of the groove, the arc of swing of the router may mean that you need to position the cutter in the groove before you switch the router on.
- It is important that you keep the Routerlathe clean, and an occasional spray of light oil on the rails on which the router

Fig. 128 The finished pierced barely twist. It took a total of ten passes using two different cutters. There has been no sanding.

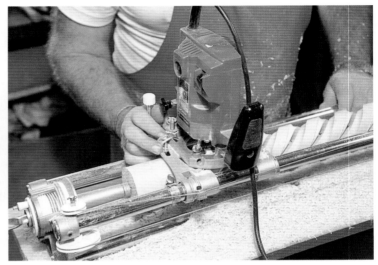

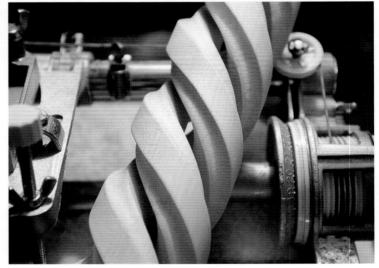

carriage runs will help in achieving clean jump-free passages.
- A strong word of warning: all routers produce fine cuttings and dust so a mask is essential. They also make noise, to a degree that is beyond the danger level for most ears and which in the long term is damaging to all ears. Ear defenders are therefore a MUST at all times that the router is running.

CONCLUSION

It has to be said that hand-cut barley twists look superb and always generate admiration. Hand-cut pierced barley twists look amazing; but some of the patterns of pierced twist that can be produced with both the full copy lathes and with the Routerlathe can only be described as stunning! Even further, I do not believe that we can now produce fluting or reeding by hand, particularly if it has a rope twist to it. We just have to turn to machines, and anything that makes it easier to achieve good looking results is welcomed in abundance!

16

FINISHING

The point has already been made that sanding spindles is basically not accepted practice, but perhaps we need to qualify this. There are many turners who absolutely decry the use of abrasives on any form of turning, maintaining that tooling skills should be developed to such a high level that the finish achieved is so fine that it does not need *any* sanding. But we all make mistakes at some time or other; and then there are occasions when it is almost impossible to achieve a satisfactory finish on the wood we are using without some 'artificial' aids.

The range of finishing problems that the spindle turner encounters are nowhere near as great as those that the bowl turner has to face. In the hollowing-out stage of bowl turning it is difficult to avoid cutting up from under the ends of unsupported end grain. In spindle turning there is absolutely no occasion when this should happen, because we are always cutting downhill along the grain, or directly into end grain; so you should never have fluffy, torn grain to contend with (unless repairing the product of a copy attachment).

It is certainly true that with the right tool, nicely sharpened and used in the correct manner, it should be possible for the spindle turner to achieve a good finish straight off the tool. Indeed, if proper bevel contact is maintained – and this is *always* possible in turning spindles – you should achieve a burnished finish that can actually be degraded with abrasives. If any sanding is necessary, do it by hand and work along the grain using fine grades of abrasive papers.

FINISHING PROBLEMS

There are three finishing problems that you might encounter in between-centres work. The first is known as ripple finish and is due to flexing or vibration. Hopefully you will have spotted this when it first occurs, and it really does have to be cut away as no amount of treatment with abrasives will get rid of it.

The second problem is the hallmark of carelessness: the accidental creation of a spiral groove where an edge or a corner of the blade has caught and either bruised or cut a spiral. This too usually has to be cut away, and only the lightest of bruising can be removed with sandpaper.

The third problem may sometimes be abraded away. With softer, fibrous woods you can get a fibre or two rolling away leaving a short indentation along the lie of the grain. This will always occur on the apex of a convex curve, usually a bead or an ovolo. By altering the edge presentation you may be able to cut it away – although sometimes this may mean reshaping all the other copies. It may be possible to sand along the grain and to hide the blemish sufficiently well for it to be acceptable, particularly if it can be positioned and fixed such that the errant facet is hidden.

THE DISADVANTAGES OF ABRASIVES

The problem with using abrasives to clean spindles is that they invariably soften corners and round over edges; this may be only slightly, but it is the crisp edges to features that make the spindle attractive.

If just a light touch-up is required, then never use whole sheets of abrasive papers. You may find it useful to keep a jam-jar containing a number of strips and dowels of wood and short lengths of narrow-gauge hosepipe of appropriate sizes and diameters, round which the abrasives may be wrapped; in this way they can be made to fit precisely into or onto the feature that you are cleaning.

Now we come up against the real problem: any cabinet maker or carpenter will tell you that you always sand along the grain, however, you cannot always do that on some spindle detail. Coves have to be sanded with the lathe turning and with the abrasives rubbing across the grain, so in the process of smoothing the whole you may make rings of abrasive scratches. If you then try to remove these with finer grits, you are soon well down the road to losing all definition to the turning.

When looking at the cutting of twists it was proposed that flap wheels could be used to clean out the troughs. When they work along the grain they perform well, but they are altogether too crude for use on most spindle features.

There really isn't any alternative to proper tooling!

USING SANDING SEALER

So if you can't sand, what about sanding sealer? Of course you may use it and then lightly smooth with abrasives, but again you have to ask yourself if it is necessary. Much of what the spindle turner makes will be in pine, oak, mahogany and beech. Pine burnishes under the bevel to a very fine finish, as can beech; these certainly do not need sealer. Most of the denser imported hardwoods also burnish well. The mahogany we use today can be very variable and some does have an open texture; these you may well wish to seal. Oak is naturally of an open texture, and does not bevel-burnish particularly well; but then the natural character of oak and the way it is used usually makes broad decoration and open texture wholly acceptable. Thus sealed oak would look almost unnatural. Each of the other woods we use will fit within these three patterns.

BURNISHING

Bowl turners burnish their work by holding a bunch of turnings against it while it is spinning. Spindle turners should always do this, but they may go further. Shavings burnishing is done by holding a handful of the shavings from turning against the spindle while it is rotated at medium speed. Some pressure is applied and heat is generated so a

Fig. 129 A goblet bowl being burnished by turning it against a handful of shavings.

leather or industrial glove should be worn. This burnishing will apply some 'polish' and will generally help to clean up the spindle.

The second stage of burnishing can be carried out now and may even be repeated after the piece has been stained. In this process blocks of wood are held against the rotating piece: it is best if the pieces of wood are of similar type and they should be shaped to fit particular features so as to reach into difficult corners. The burnisher block is offered up with a polished face resting on the spindle, and the axis of the burnisher's grain at right-angles to the grain axis of the spindle. Some pressure is applied, but care must be taken to ensure that the friction does not build up to fire-lighting level and scorch the wood!

STAINING AND POLISHING

Finishing really starts with the next procedure.

Reproduction furniture makers, trying to make their pieces look 'original', spend a lot of time getting the surface right. They use burnishers to achieve a 'natural' polish, particularly on areas that would normally be handled or brushed against in domestic use: the apexes of beads, handles, the front faces of drawers, and so on. A slightly darker stain is then brushed into the nooks and crannies and graded off into the more open areas; while this is still damp, the whole spindle is coated with the required colour of stain. This is left to dry. Next, a coating of black patinating wax is applied with a soft cloth. This is, however, spun on the lathe and the cloth rubs off as much of the blacking as possible, leaving only a residue in grooves and recesses. Finally the whole is polished with a beeswax-based product or finished with button or French polish.

There are basically three final finishing approaches from which to choose:

1. natural grain and colour enhancer finishes;
2. natural grain and colour changing finishes;
3. applied opaque colour finishes.

NATURAL GRAIN AND COLOUR ENHANCER FINISHES

Natural grain colour enhancers are transparent, and do not hide the grain or artificially change the colour of the timber. Usually they feed the wood with some type of oil such as turpentine or linseed, thus bringing out the natural colour. Some finishes are totally colourless; some may have a natural 'brownness'. Some are polishes which, while their oils and solvents penetrate the wood, also contain a wax or similar which will form an extremely thin surface skin. Amongst this group we have to consider beeswax compounded polishes; the browning shellac-based French and button polishes; and lathe-applied, colourless friction polishes, often melamine or cellulose based. Others may also penetrate, but their prime purpose is to build up a thicker protective skin on the surface, the main types being colourless varnishes, the most durable of which have a urethane base.

Fortunately most spindles are not subject to hot plates and alcohol spillages, so we can use almost any finish without fear of staining or degradation. Of course if the 'spindle' is to be a goblet that will be used for liquids it will need a sealing surface such as a polyurethane varnish.

NATURAL GRAIN AND COLOUR CHANGING FINISHES

There are many decorative spindles made in which the grain pattern and figure of the

153

wood are retained but the colour is changed. Sometimes the change is to a so-called 'natural wood' colour, but on others there is a more fundamental change because it is dyed to a pigmented spectrum colour. There are two types of process involved: in one, the colouring is in the medium which is a transparent varnish or lacquer; the other group usually involves dyeing or staining the wood with a semi-transparent colouring agent and then applying one of the transparent finishes.

Chemical Processes

There is less interest today – except amongst a small group of restorers and reproduction furniture makers – in the use of chemical processes, which do anything from slightly modify to change fundamentally the natural colour of the wood. The reason for their fall from grace lies in the difficulty of use: they are all messy, and some are potentially hazardous. They do, however, produce extremely good results which have a particular depth and character. They include fuming, chemical staining, liming and also bleaching techniques.

References

If you are interested in studying further the intricacies of traditional colouring and finishing you might like to refer to two excellent texts: *Staining and Polishing* by Charles H. Hayward, published by Unwin Paperbacks; and Frederick Ougton's *The Complete Manual of Wood Finishing* published by Stobart & Son Ltd; together they should provide all the information that you will ever need.

OPAQUE COLOUR FINISHES

The third group of finishing approaches uses opaque substances which totally hide the grain and colour of the wood. There are still two 'sub-sets'. One group comprises the 'wood'-coloured lacquers and so-called 'varnishes', whose opacity is such that in fact they virtually hide the nature of the wood itself, although their colours are supposed to simulate a 'natural' wood colour. They are most widely used on flooring and other areas of internal woodwork and were much used in the twenties and thirties. Today they are likely to be of only marginal interest to the turner. At one time some pine furniture was treated in this way because pine was considered to be the most inferior of all furniture-making timbers, and it was therefore lacquered to a dark oak, or some other colour.

The second sub-set of opaque finishes is obviously normal 'spectrum coloured' household paint.

If colour staining is your choice you will undoubtedly be into food dyes, or the excellent water-based, wood-dye product range from Liebron. If you opt for opaque paint the choice is open-ended, and you may be involved in brushing, air brushing or full-blown spraying. Should you wish to follow this route, look at the work and acquire the books of American Merryl Saylan or English Jan Sanders – their work is stunning. Beyond this you may at some time wish to penetrate the art world of decorated furniture where enamels or even artists' paint may be used.

Student quality tubes of acrylic colours can give very exciting results. Acrylics have one huge advantage. With the careful use of a hair-drier or a heat gun set on low, a layer of wet colour can be dried ready for overpainting in only seconds. Also masking tape allows you to produce hard edges with no bleed.

CONCLUSION

Clearly with such a range of options, and many more particular approaches that have not even been mentioned, finishing is a vast subject and there are several

Fig. 130 Not a spindle, but a wooden duck. The colour is students' grade acrylic paint: it is easy to apply to wood (using acrylic white primer) and can be very quickly dried with a hot-air gun.

books which deal with this aspect of wood-work alone.

The type of work you wish to do will, inevitably, set a broad direction. If your first love is furniture, you may look towards restoration, reproduction and traditional techniques, in which case you will probably wish to brew your own stains and finishes using chemicals and powders. Many of the proprietary finishes are very good, but matching the colour of an existing piece will soon push you down the do-it-yourself route. Bichromate of potash, tannic acid, aniline dyes and fume cupboards will be your lot. You, too, will be buying up old '78' records and dissolving the black shellac in methylated spirits to make good ebonizing materials; and many other wheezes that you will find in aforementioned books on finishing.

You will probably get into fuming, where oak is blackened by enclosing it in a large plastic bag with bowls of 880 ammonia; or into bleaching with oxalic acid and chloride compounds. You may wish to experiment with strong domestic bleaches, or staining with garden lawn-moss killer (the iron content reacts beautifully with ammonia).

On the other hand you may be quite happy to use the available preparatory finishes. Here you will find that the water-based dyes are much more permanent than some of the spirit-based products. Many modern 'quick' methods are very good: pre-formulated French polish is much less tedious than making up your own traditional brews; and button polish is a wonderful, even easier-to-use finish for 'traditional' wood work. Moreover, the materials for almost anything you can think of doing are available, and expert advice can always be found.

Have fun!

USEFUL ADDRESSES

These are the addresses of some of the sources and contacts used regularly by the author:

Association of Woodturners of Great Britain,
Hon Sec. Peter Einig,
Keeper's Cottage,
Lee,
Ellesmere,
Shropshire SY12 9AE.

Axminster Power Tool Centre
(machinery, power and hand tools, chucks and drive centres)
Chard Street,
Axminster,
Devon EX13 5DZ.

Poolewood Equipment Ltd
(lathes and machinery)
Crown House,
Traffic Street,
Nottingham NG2 1NE.

Hapfo Pollards Ltd
(copy and automatic lathes)
1 Water Hall Industrial Estate,
Salford,
Milton Keynes MK17 8AZ.

Tewkesbury Saw
(machinery, copy lathes, and saw blades)
Newton Trading Estate,
Tewkesbury,
Gloucestershire GL20 8JG.

Trend Routing and Cutting Tools Ltd
(normally through their stockist network)
Penfold Works,
Imperial Way,
Watford,
Herts WD2 4YF.

Techlink Enterprises Ltd
(indexing heads and fluter devices)
(Tony Bunce)
17 Hazell Way,
Stoke Poges,
Slough,
Berks SL2 4BW.

Ashley Isles (Edge Tools) Ltd
(carving and turning tools and buffing equipment)
East Kirkby,
Spilsby,
Lincolnshire PE23 4DD.

Robert Sorby
(turning tools and chucks; normally through dealers)
Athol Road,
Sheffield S8 0PA.

Yandle and Sons Ltd
(timber, tools and finishes)
Hurst Works,
Martock,
Somerset TA12 6JU.

John Boddy Fine Tool Store Ltd
(timber, accessories and tools)
Riverside Sawmills,
Boroughbridge,
North Yorkshire YO5 9LJ.

Craft Supplies Ltd
(timber, accessories and tools)
The Mill,
Miller's Dale,
Nr. Buxton,
Derbyshire SK17 8SN

Isaac Lord Ltd
(timber, machines, tools and
ironmongery)
185 Desborough Road,
High Wycombe,
Bucks HP11 2QN.

Ian Durrant
(OCA chucks and off-centre advice)
76 Sheering Lower Road,
Sawbridgeworth,
Hertfordshire CM21 9LH.

Jan Sanders
(books, videos and information on
colouring)
Potters Cottage,
Northay,
Chard,
Somerset TA20 3DN.

Simbles
(engineering supplies, tool buffing
equipment)
The Broadway,
Queen's Road,
Watford,
Herts WD1 2LD.

E. W. Lucas Ltd
(power tools)
253–257 Washwood Heath Road,
Birmingham B8 1RL.

Brimarc Associates
(Tormek, vices and devices)
Unit 8,
Ladbroke Park,
Millers Road,
Warwick CV34 5AE.

Stobart Davies Ltd
(woodworking books)
Priory House,
21 Priory Street,
Hertford,
Herts SG14 1RN.

Nexus Plans Service
(furniture and general woodworking
plans)
Nexus Specialist Publications,
Nexus House,
Boundary Way,
Hemel Hempstead,
Herts HP2 7ST.

Peter Blake
(supplies and gallery sales)
Burford House Woodturning Centre,
Burford House Gardens,
Burford,
Tenbury Wells,
Worcs WR15 8HQ.

Thank you for your services past and
present!

Hugh O'Neill
Myttons Craft Centre,
Boraston,
Tenbury Wells,
Worcs WR15 8LH.

INDEX